In the Steps of
the Great American Entomologist
Frank
Eugene
Lutz

In the Steps of
the Great American Entomologist

Frank
Eugene
Lutz

ᴣᴀ

by John Pallister

Illustrations by Kathleen Elgin

ᴣᴀ

M Evans
Lanham • New York • Boulder • Toronto • Plymouth, UK

M. Evans
An imprint of The Rowman & Littlefield Publishing Group, Inc.
4501 Forbes Boulevard, Suite 200, Lanham, Maryland 20706
http://www.rlpgtrade.com

10 Thornbury Road, Plymouth PL6 7PP, United Kingdom

Distributed by National Book Network

British Library Cataloguing in Publication Information Available

Library of Congress Cataloging-in-Publication Data Available

ISBN 13: 978-1-59077-364-2 (pbk: alk. paper)

♾™ The paper used in this publication meets the minimum requirements of American National Standard for Information Sciences—Permanence of Paper for Printed Library Materials, ANSI/NISO Z39.48-1992.

Printed in the United States of America

Design by Robin Sherwood

I acknowledge with appreciation the assistance Jean Burns gave to me in the writing of this book.

I also acknowledge the help of Dr. Herbert Ruckes, Dr. Harold Anthony, and Miss Alice Gray of the American Museum of Natural History, and of Miss Anne Lutz in providing important useful information.

Contents

1. A Boy's World 9

2. A New Venture 25

3. Museum Hall and
   Tropical Forest 38

4. Insects See the Light 54

5. The Stingless Bees of Panama 67

6. Bringing Insect Life
   to the Public 78

7. A Lot of Insects 93

   Nature Projects You Can Do 107

   Bibliography 128

1
A Boy's World

Frank cast his line and stretched out on the grass to wait for a bite. As he lay there on his side, a patch of color caught his eye. One moment the brilliantly colored caterpillar was lying completely still along a leaf of the milkweed plant near him. The next moment it was arching itself up as though stabbed. Then it started stretching and squirming frantically. It seemed to be straining desperately to crawl forward. But something seemed to be holding it back.

The boy moved closer. What was happening? The stretching and straining continued. Then the creature's body puffed up. Suddenly, just behind its head, the skin burst open. Frank held his breath. Now it's done it, he thought. The poor thing really has split apart at the seams.

But nothing of the sort had happened. The caterpillar just went on wriggling as energetically as ever.

Now, at last, it was moving ahead a bit. The split down its back widened as the damp caterpillar emerged. Frank watched, fascinated. A half hour later it had freed itself completely. He sat up, astonished. For the first time in his life, Frank Eugene Lutz had seen a caterpillar shed its skin.

Gathering up his fishing gear, he started for home. It was shortly after noon—very early in the day for him to be going home. Usually there was too much happening outdoors for him to want to stay inside, particularly during the summer vacation. Whole days could be spent fishing down at the creek near town—and that was probably his favorite pastime. But he also loved to go hiking with some of his classmates through the green Pennsylvania mountains near the town of Bloomsburg, where he was born in 1879. And he enjoyed hunting, or visiting his grandparents' farm.

This particular day, however, Frank was in a hurry to get home. He wanted to find out more about what he had just seen. It was, he knew, too early for his father and older brother to be at home. But he knew he could probably find what he wanted in a book on biology his brother had used at school.

Upstairs in his brother's room, Frank found the book he was looking for. He quickly leafed through it until he found the section on insects. Then he started to read. What he had seen back there on the milkweed leaf was no rare event. In fact, caterpillars, he learned, shed their skins several times as they grow bigger. The caterpillar he'd been watching would cast off its skin five times within a two-week period

10

before becoming fully grown. Then it would be ready for the next stage of development: the change into a chrysalis. Seeking out the underside of a strong leaf, or some other protected place, the caterpillar would spin a pad of silk from its mouth and fasten itself by its "tail-end" to this pad. Then, as it hung there, the transformation would take place. The caterpillar would discard its skin for the last time, becoming completely encased in a translucent green capsule flecked with gold. From this chrysalis would emerge, some 10 to 15 days later, the splendid, brilliant monarch butterfly.

As Frank read on, a new world opened up for him. He had never thought insects were so complicated and interesting. As a matter of fact, he had never given them much thought at all. He probably knew as much about insects as any other boy his age. He knew the names of quite a number of different species. He knew a good deal about which insects make the best fish bait. And he did know that insects change their form as they get older, although he had never seen it happen. The book told him the names of the four stages of development of most insects' lives—egg, larva, pupa, and adult. The creature he knew as a caterpillar was really the larval stage of the monarch butterfly. When it changed into a chrysalis it would be in the pupal stage.

From that day on, Frank had a new interest. And since he had always loved nature and the outdoors, no one was surprised that Frank had become fascinated by one more aspect of the natural world.

He also liked to read. He tried to find some books that would tell him more about insect habits, but there was almost nothing in the school library that explained any more than his brother's textbook. He had always done very well at school. In fact, his marks were so good that his mother and father had been forced to have serious second thoughts about the future they originally had in mind for the boy.

They had planned for him to work with his father as an insurance agent, which required no college education. But he was such a bright student that, although they could barely afford it, they decided Frank must go to college. And so, as the 1880's became the 1890's and the boy grew, Mr. and Mrs. Lutz saved whatever money they could, wondering all the while what career or profession Frank might eventually choose. He was particularly good in mathematics, and so they considered occupations that might put this aptitude to work. No one, not even Frank, ever considered the possibility that there might be a relationship between his interest in living creatures and his future career.

By the time Frank was ready for college, he was considerably confused. So many of his high school subjects fascinated him—especially his courses in the natural sciences and mathematics—that he couldn't decide what to select for his major field of study in college.

It was then that Mr. Lutz came forward with some advice. He believed a college education should be practical. He heard that the big-city offices of insurance companies were hiring mathematicians as actuaries and, furthermore, were paying them very handsome salaries. So it seemed quite reasonable to him to suggest that Frank study mathematics.

In the fall of 1896 Frank went off to Haverford College, a school for men near Philadelphia. And there for the first two years he lived the life of any other typical college student. He studied mathematics, as his father had wanted, and achieved good grades. He joined in many of the campus activities. At vacation time, he took odd jobs in his home town to help pay his next year's tuition. It was during one of those summer vacations that an incident occurred that clearly indicated the direction his later life would take.

Toward the end of an August afternoon Mr. Lutz returned home from a business trip he'd made to a town some 30 miles away. He was hot and tired from the trip—those were still the horse and buggy days. But he was full of excitement about something he had seen some miles back. He had been driving along a lonely country road when he saw ahead of him what seemed at first to be some strange blight on the green landscape. On one entire side of a hill, every single tree had been stripped completely bare of leaves. As he got closer he saw what was causing the terrible destruction. Swarming all over that hillside were thousands upon thousands of weird stick-like insects, each about four inches long. It looked as though the entire hillside was being eaten up.

Frank was fascinated by his father's description. The insects must be walking sticks. Yet walking sticks, he knew, were fairly rare insects. Certainly he had never heard of their being seen in large numbers. This was something he had to see for himself.

Following his father's directions, he found the hill. The sight he beheld gave him goose-flesh and made him shiver. He found it at once frightening and weird-ly beautiful. It was frightening not because of any danger, but because of the way in which the scene suddenly suggested to him nature's strange and startling capacity for mystery.

Suddenly a new thought occurred to him. Just a few days ago he had seen a picture of a walking stick in an advertisement by a New York firm that supplied specimens and equipment for scientific study. Hurriedly, he sent off a telegram to the director of the firm asking whether he would like to purchase some walking stick specimens. And if so, how much would he pay?

The reply was prompt. Yes, indeed the director was interested. In fact he would be willing to pay as much as a penny apiece since walking sticks were quite uncommon.

Frank flew into action. In no time at all he hitched the horse and was heading back in the direction of the hill. A penny per insect was a very good price indeed. Obviously the firm expected that, working very hard, he might possibly get 15 or 20 specimens—certainly no more.

The trees on the hill were as bare as though it were mid-winter. But the hillside itself was alive with insects. They were on the ground and in the trees. Frank had brought along several large flour sacks in which he planned to put as many as he could fit in.

The problem was how to get them into the sacks. He started to pick them up one by one and put them in, but he quickly decided that that method would take forever. Then he had an idea. He would hold a flour sack open underneath a tree and hit the branches

with a stick. With each hit, a nickel's worth or a dime's worth of walking sticks would fall off and drop into the sack. When a sack was filled he tied it up and started on the next. It didn't take too long before all the sacks were filled to the top with a mass of swarming, crawling walking sticks.

Now what should he do? He hadn't thought of asking whether the firm in New York wanted them dead or alive. He'd better ship them off, he thought, just as soon as possible and hope for the best. On the way home, he bought a large carton, stuffed the sacks into it, took it over to the railroad station and sent it by express to its destination.

With the carton went a letter. He had not counted the contents, he wrote, but was sure that there must be well over 2,000 specimens. However, he would take $15 for the lot.

It wasn't long after that that a check for $15 made out to Frank Eugene Lutz arrived. This was the first money Frank earned through working with insects. Years later, when he met the manager of the New York firm he had sent the insects to, he learned that the carton had been brought directly into the manager's office and opened up there. To everybody's horror, wave upon wave of exceedingly lively walking sticks flowed out all over the office, under the doors, into the main showroom and clambered all over the display cases. It took quite some time to get things back to normal.

Back at college in his junior year, Frank was ready to make a decision about his career. He definitely did not want to become an actuary, no matter how high the salary. He would like to be a physician. He switched his major from mathematics to biology in preparation for the new career he planned.

But as the end of his senior year drew closer, he realized that he did not have enough money to continue his studies. He would have to get a job right after graduation and save as much as he could. Then he could go on to medical school. What kind of work could he do? The only thing he could think of was actuarial work. His two years of mathematics training would probably qualify him.

The president of his college gave him a letter of introduction to the head of the actuarial department of a large insurance company in Philadelphia, and so Frank went to the man's office for an interview. All went well, until he was asked to take a penmanship test.

"Ouch!" he recalled later. "That old fellow's scorn at my handwriting was most impressive. He sent me out of his office in no time at all."

Thoroughly discouraged, he didn't know where to turn. Then his biology teacher came to his rescue. During the summer vacation, Professor Pratt taught at a biological laboratory operated by the Brooklyn Institute of Arts and Sciences in Cold Spring Harbor, New York. The director of the laboratory was Dr. Charles B. Davenport of the University of Chicago, a distinguished scientist and one of the fathers of the science of genetics in America.

Dr. Davenport then was doing pioneer work in the new science of biometry. Biometry was the application of mathematics to biology and seemed an ideal field for a student whose college courses were in exactly

those subjects. Professor Pratt thought Frank might apply for a scholarship to study at Chicago with Dr. Davenport. In the meantime, he could get a job at Cold Spring Harbor. It was a summer resort as well, and college boys could always be used to wait on tables in the hotels and restaurants there.

It was a good idea and Frank was delighted to find this solution to his problem.

After graduation, he went to Cold Spring Harbor, on the North Shore of Long Island. When he wasn't carrying trays of food and clearing dirty dishes from dining-room tables, he worked on his first scientific paper. He had to present a report on some original research in order to qualify for the scholarship that he had now set his heart on. Being at the seashore, he decided it would be convenient to write about a sea creature: the scallop. First, he collected great numbers of scallops. Then came the real work.

Hour after hour he sat, patiently and painstakingly counting the number of grooves on each scallop shell. Hour after hour he checked and re-checked until his eyes ached. Some 500 scallops were studied—a total of 1,000 shells in all—before he felt he had enough data. Now came some mathematical calculations. Then he wrote his paper. Most shells, he had found, were almost exactly alike. But the number of ridges might vary slightly. It was about these variations that he wrote.

Many years later, he was to say that he didn't think his little paper (it was only 18 lines long, not counting the title) "greatly advanced the cause of science." However, it did win him the scholarship to Chicago.

The scholarship covered only tuition. Dr. Davenport and his wife let him stay in their spare bedroom, and he used his newly developed skill as a waiter to earn whatever money he needed for board.

Two years in Chicago, and he had his master's degree. He spent another summer earning some money at Cold Spring Harbor, this time helping to get rid of some of Long Island's mosquitoes. It was one of the first mosquito control projects in the United States, and Frank Lutz's share in it earned him enough for a 10-month trip to Europe.

In England he was the first American student of Professor Karl Pearson, the mathematician credited with founding biometry. Pearson was then applying statistical methods to the study of heredity.

After a few months of further study in Berlin he returned home, and went back to the University of Chicago to start work on his Ph.D. For his research project he decided to do an analysis of the measurements of the legs, wings, and other parts of thousands of crickets.

And then Dr. Davenport himself suggested the next step in Frank Lutz's career. A completely new venture was being launched at Cold Spring Harbor. It was probably the most exciting thing in American science at the time—1904. Would he like to be part of it?

Would he? He knew it was the chance of a lifetime.

2
A New Venture

The village of Cold Spring Harbor was once, many years ago, a busy whaling port. From its piers, scores of sailing ships set out, returning long months later with their precious cargo. It was a lively, colorful place in those days, crowded with sailors from foreign lands. Indeed, so many languages were heard up and down the main street that it became known as "Bedlam Street."

Then other people began to discover the delights of Cold Spring Harbor. Gradually, a number of large, handsome houses appeared in the area. And the small town changed from a thriving whaling port into a favorite seaside resort for wealthy New Yorkers and their families.

Frank Lutz returned to this picturesque spot one day in May 1904. Although he had spent two summers here, he now looked at the village as though he

25

had never set eyes on it. Everything was different. He was no longer a student. There would be no more waiting on tables, no more gratefully accepting the hospitality of the Davenports. He was on his own now, launched on his career at last, after eight long years of study. And tomorrow would be his first day of real work.

His destination was not the town itself, but an estate just beyond it. As he came up the road, Frank took in the peaceful country setting. It contrasted strangely with the tingle of excitement he felt at being part of this new venture.

A brand-new research laboratory, to be known as the Station for Experimental Evolution, had just been set up by the marvelously wealthy Carnegie Institution of Washington, D.C. Under Davenport, who was its director, a staff of scientists would be able to devote themselves full time to conducting experiments in heredity and genetics. They would be able to follow their experiments wherever they might lead, a tremendously exciting prospect. With the Carnegie Institution behind them, there was no imaginable limit to what they might discover!

Frank entered a gleaming new building that hummed with activity. New equipment was everywhere—some of it already on the tables and shelves, but most of it still in unpacked cartons and crates that cluttered the corridors. Staff members dashed past him, carrying armloads of books or racks of small glass vials. Some cradled small glass greenhouses in their arms, while others awkwardly hefted large wire cages.

It was a thrilling place for a young scientist to be. Here in this building, a group of men were about to begin a great scientific adventure. They were about to set out to explore a completely uncharted field—the newly discovered field of what today is called genetics, the science of heredity. They would, by conducting experiments on all sorts of living things (mammals, birds, insects, plants), be seeking answers to such basic, vital questions as: Why do members of a family—human or otherwise—resemble each other and yet vary so much? How do these differences and likenesses come about? Which is more important, heredity or environment? How does each work? What exactly *is* heredity?

All sorts of scientists were needed. They would conduct experiments in many areas. They all looked forward to working with Dr. Davenport, who was well known for his pioneering work in this new science of genetics. He had gathered a staff of specialists in biology, zoology, botany, psychology. Because Frank Lutz had done some work with insects during his years in graduate school, Davenport had asked his student to come along as an entomologist.

His job would be to set up a series of experiments to explore the laws of heredity as they worked on insects. This would really be breaking new ground. Why, it was only four years earlier that the scientific world had become aware of the laws of heredity.

It was an Austrian monk, Gregor Mendel, who first discovered that certain characteristics are handed down from generation to generation in a regular pattern. Mendel published the results of his experiments on the garden pea and other plants in 1866, but for more than 30 years his paper on the laws of heredity went undiscovered by scientists. Not until 1900 was his work publicized. Only then did scientists around the world begin additional experiments to gain a deeper understanding of one of nature's most fascinating mysteries.

Entomology was a new science, too. Only in the last few years had scientists begun to specialize in the insect corner of the biological world. Lutz had had no specific courses in entomology at Haverford or at the University of Chicago. What was known about insect life was taught as part of other courses, by professors who were biologists or perhaps zoologists. At the turn of the century the biological sciences were just beginning to develop into specialties.

His work at the Station would be just the kind of challenge Lutz liked. But there were drawbacks to being a pioneer. To begin with, he had no idea what insect to choose for his experiments. Until he overcame that particular obstacle, he couldn't even start to work.

Feeling a little apprehensive, he sat down to draw up a list of "musts." First and most important, he needed an insect that would reproduce rapidly. To study heredity meant studying not just parents, children, grandchildren, and perhaps a fourth generation; it meant studying generation after generation of a family—perhaps a hundred or even more generations. So an insect that lived too long or took too long to mature would be no good at all for his purposes. He needed an insect that produced a new generation frequently.

Again, the insect he was looking for would have to adjust well to being kept in captivity. It must also be easy and preferably, not too expensive to feed. And lastly, the subject of his experiments would have to be plentiful so he could select from thousands, if necessary, to find the small variations he was to study.

There was one promising prospect. The year before, while visiting friends in Boston, he had met a scientist who was doing some experiments with *Drosophila*, those tiny red-eyed fruitflies which can often be seen around bananas or other fruit. He remembered hearing that they matured very quickly —it took only about 10 days or two weeks for them to produce a new generation, and they reproduced all year round. If this were so, he would be able to raise 25 generations of *Drosophila* in one year. To study that many human generations would take 750 years!

He had to find out more. Perhaps Drosophila was the insect for him. Off went a letter to Boston.

One day about a week later he arrived at his laboratory to find an odd-shaped package. He unwrapped it, removing layer after layer of paper, cardboard, and soft cotton. Inside was a jar that was alive with hundreds of tiny brownish flies. Attached to it was a note: " Herewith some members of the finest New England families to ensure your work of the best possible start. I recommend them highly."

But he needed to get thousands before he could begin. That would be fairly easy. He placed some bananas in jars out-of-doors near the laboratory, and in a few days he had a perfectly adequate collection of Long Island fruitflies.

Then one morning he sat down at his desk in the laboratory, very carefully transferred one of the tiny flies from its glass "home" into a special saucer-like container, and, magnifying glass in hand, examined every minute segment of it. A second followed, then a

What he was looking for was a particular fruitfly that would be different, in some special way, from all the others. This unique character, known as a variation, would be the starting point for his studies of heredity.

third, and a fourth. The search was on.

It was a long search. One by one he examined the tiny creatures. The figures climbed from 10 . . . to 50 . . . to 100 . . . to 500 . . .

Finally he saw it. There under the lens was the answer to his search—a fruitfly that had something different about it. Right at the tip of one tiny wing— barely visible even under the magnifying glass—was a minute speck. It was a vein that he hadn't seen on any other *Drosophila*. It was all he needed. Now at last he could begin his experiment.

First, he selected a perfectly normal mate for his little prize specimen. Then he put husband and wife into a jar together with a piece of over-ripe banana to serve as food for their offspring. On the banana he put a piece of crumpled paper to give the female a good foothold when she came to lay eggs. Now he waited. In a few days, right on the surface of the banana, the first white eggs appeared—so tiny they couldn't be seen without a lens. Two days more and the eggs hatched into squirming little white larvae. Then a long week went by before these maggots retreated into their shells for the pupal phase.

Now four more days and the straw-colored pupae started splitting open. Out of them emerged the first young adults. Lutz went for his magnifying glass. Then, one by one, he examined them.

Every one he looked at seemed completely normal. But it was too soon yet to say anything definite. The mother of this batch would go on laying eggs for almost a month—some 200 in all would be a good average.

Within the next few days, a second batch of brothers and sisters emerged. Then a third, then a fourth. By the time he had examined the sixth batch there was no longer any doubt: all the offspring looked perfectly normal. This was what he had expected. According to the Mendelian laws of heredity, the offspring of this mating would appear normal. It was in some of *their* offspring (that is, the grandchildren of the original couple) that the abnormal trait would reappear.

This is exactly what happened. And now from this second generation on, a whole series of different experiments was to take place.

In the years that followed he was able, by careful breeding, to produce entire new strains of *Drosophila* where every single member had abnormal wings. In some strains, the veins might be shorter than normal. In others, he could increase the abnormality until there were extra veins all over the wing. In still others he could even reduce the number of veins.

"However, the latter strain," he wrote in his report, "is manifestly not fitted to maintain itself. The wings, deprived of the support of the veins, droop and catch

33

in the food of the insect, resulting in the insect's death."

Then one day he decided to find out what would happen to his race of extra-veined flies if they were turned loose in nature with normal plain-winged individuals.

On May 2, he noted in his journal, "I released in a large battery-jar an equal number of flies from one of my extra-veined strains and from one of my plain-winged strains."

Two and a half weeks later, on May 19, he noted: "Only 26 per cent of the flies in the jar showed extra veins and these veins were not as pronounced as those of the original 50 per cent."

By June 23, seven weeks after the start of the experiment, "Only one per cent showed any trace of extra veins."

It was extraordinary. What could have happened? He would have to start at the beginning—and this time watch every moment.

Into a jar he put one normal female fly and two males—a normal one and an extra-veined one. He settled down to wait.

The curious dance began. First one male, then the other went into the special dance that marks the beginning of fruitfly courtship. Around the jar the trio flew in their strange little ritual. The males flitted their wings in front of the female, flying now up and down, now from side to side, doing their best to show off. An hour went by. Then the female made her choice. It was the normal fly.

Lutz got up. It was very interesting, of course. But one test didn't prove a thing. He would have to repeat the experiment, using different flies each time. Over and over again, in the days that followed, he put different *Drosophila* through the test. And time after time, the result was the same: the female, even if she herself was of the extra-veined strain, invariably chose a plain-winged fly as her mate.

Quite clearly, the female *Drosophila*—if given a choice—simply did not like his extra-veined strain of flies. Why not, he wondered. Could she perhaps actually see the extra vein? And was the sight of it so unattractive that she would have no part of the extra-veined male?

He would try to find out. The extra veins were at the extreme tips of the wings. Using his delicate laboratory instruments Lutz snipped off the wing tips of some of the extra-veined and some ordinary, plain-winged males. Now both abnormal and normal flies looked exactly alike.

He was ready to test them again. Using a specially compartmented jar he put in one female and two clipped-winged males, one of which had originally had extra veins. A second time the test was repeated, using three different flies. Then a third, a tenth. . . . The result was invariably the same. The female went to the *Drosophila* that had been normal.

Obviously, it couldn't be the sight of the extra veins that invariably displeased the female flies. There was something else about his pedigreed males that the females didn't like. Trying to find out what it might be would require more study and more experiments. But it might well be interesting. Perhaps that might be his next project.

But his days at Cold Spring Harbor were numbered. One of the other scientists at the Station, Professor Henry E. Crampton, had been appointed curator of invertebrate zoology at the American Museum of Natural History in New York City. He needed a good entomologist for his growing department, which was concerned with the very numerous category of animals without backbones. He thought of the promising young scientist at Cold Spring Harbor.

Lutz hesitated when first offered the job. It sounded tempting. The Museum would be a wonderful place to work. It had grown steadily since its founding 40 years earlier, and was now world famous for its great collections and as a pioneer in research and exhibition techniques. Yet Lutz had become so absorbed with his *Drosophila* he didn't want to abandon them. His work at the Station still fascinated him.

"Bring your *Drosophila* with you," Professor Crampton said. That settled it—that, and the promise of thousands of varieties of other insects to study. The Lutz family—now consisting of Frank himself, his wife Anna, and one child—moved, complete with swarms of *Drosophila,* to New York City.

There Lutz continued for a time with certain of the *Drosophila* experiments he'd been doing. But he never was able to solve the particular mystery of what it was about his extra-veined males that made females reject them.

It remains a mystery to this day, although work on other subjects has suggested a possible solution. It is likely that there was not just one abnormality in those flies but others, too, so minute they escaped detection by Lutz. Other scientists have continued

36

breeding *Drosophila* to study other problems in genetics. Some of the most famous of these experiments were performed by Dr. Thomas Hunt Morgan on the descendants of a white-eyed fly given to him by Lutz. But no one returned to the problem of the extra-veined flies.

3
Museum Hall and Tropical Forest

Early one March morning in the year 1909, Frank Lutz got off a trolley on Manhattan's Central Park West. He walked a few yards down 77th Street and then paused to look up at the great building he was about to enter. With its towers and turrets and massive stone staircase, he had always thought it looked like a castle from a story book.

Today would be his first day of work here. He was, quite naturally, a little nervous. But more than anything he was tremendously thrilled at the thought of being part of the American Museum of Natural History. Some of the most famous naturalists of the day were on the Museum's staff. Now he, Frank E. Lutz, A.B., A.M., Ph.D., was about to become a part of that illustrious group. He would have the title of Assistant Curator, Department of Invertebrate Zoology.

He climbed the stone staircase and went up to the building's top floor. He found Professor Crampton, the department head, waiting to welcome him in his study.

Together they went to the Hall of Insect Life, the large exhibit room for the general public. Lutz remembered the first time he had seen it four years ago. It had just been newly opened and everything about it—from the exhibits to the freshly painted walls—was bright and shiny new. He had stood rooted at the entrance to the Hall, speechless with wonder.

He remembered, too, the very first time he visited the Museum. It had been during his first summer at Cold Spring Harbor. He had gotten up extra early on a day off to travel to the Museum in New York. Once there, he had spent several hours wandering systematically through its halls. He had been astounded at the wealth of animal, vegetable, and mineral life on display there.

He had gone back many times after that, in the months he was at Cold Spring Harbor as a student, and in the years he was entomologist at the Station there. But of all the Museum's exhibits, the one that had always fascinated him most was the Hall of Insect Life.

It was a breathtaking sight for an entomologist—a fabulous treasurehouse of "jewels" from every corner of the globe.

To start with, there was the most spectacular collection of butterflies he had ever seen—5,000 glorious specimens from every part of North America and every other continent in the world. There was one of the unbelievably beautiful morphos of South America with wings of iridescent brilliant blue. From India came the strange *Kallima inachis*. With its wings spread it was a striking blue-orange-brown creature, but when it folded its wings, and only the undersurfaces could be seen, it was transformed into a nondescript brown object that looked for all the world like a dead leaf. There were swallowtails from all over the world: a fragile little beauty from the frozen wastes of Siberia, a great vivid green-and-brown stunner from Africa, a fantastic little creature from the East Indies with "tails" so long they looked like trailing ribbons.

Then there were beetles—case upon case of beetles from every place on earth. There was a terrifying horned Hercules beetle from Venezuela, nearly a half-foot in length. There was a weird blind cave-dweller from the Alps of Europe with thin spidery legs and a long giraffe-like neck. There was a ferocious Goliath from tropical Africa, big as a man's fist. From Africa came a dung beetle, a curious creature that forms balls of dung, lays eggs in them, and rolls them about industriously. (It was considered sacred by the ancient Egyptians.) From Australia there was a rare red-and-black jewel beetle, from South Africa came a strange, tufted short-horn, and from the United States there were somber burying beetles.

Still this wasn't all. For in yet another part of the Hall was an exhibit on insects that damage our crops; in another, termites' nests from the East Indies; and there was even a large collection of the insects and spiders of New York State.

The spiders really had no business being there since they are not insects at all, but arachnids. Nevertheless, the entomology department did encompass not only spiders but also two other "outsiders"—centipedes and millipedes. True, they are all related to insects, as are lobsters, crayfish, and crabs, since all belong to the *Arthropoda*, that group of creatures with segmented bodies, jointed legs, and an external skeleton. Within this group or *phylum,* however, are different classes. And it is to one of these, the class *Hexapoda,* that all insects belong, distinguished from the others by the following traits when adult: three pairs of legs, one or two pairs of wings, one pair of antennae, and a body that is divided into three distinct parts—head, thorax, and abdomen.

Now, in stunned surprise, Lutz heard Professor Crampton say that what was in this Insect Hall was just a small fraction of the Museum's total collection. Behind the scenes, in the offices and laboratories of the entomology department, were hundreds of thousands more.

Then Professor Crampton took Lutz through these offices and laboratories. He showed his new assistant one room that was filled with boxes. In these boxes, Crampton explained, were insects that hadn't yet been sorted out.

The new curator's heart sank a little. There seemed an awful lot of cases there, and he knew that each one contained an awful lot of insects.

The next day he and another new staff member started to count. By the time they had finished both were at a loss for words. There must be 300,000 insects all jumbled up in those cases! And most of them were without even labels—there were no clues at all as to which state or country they had come from. They would have to be sorted first by *order,* then classified by *family,* then by *genus,* then by *species.* There were 27 orders of insects, and, at that time, some 400,000 *known* species—to say nothing of hundreds of thousands more species as yet unknown and unidentified. More than nine-tenths of the world's total animal population were insects. His pet laboratory subject, the fruitfly, for instance, was a member of the order *Diptera*, the family *Drosophilidae*, the genus *Drosophila*, and the species *melanogaster*. To classify accurately the insects in all of these boxes would be a colossal task. It might take years!

The sooner they started, however, the sooner they would finish. Lutz set to work. From a storage room he took a dozen Schmitt boxes—cork-bottomed wooden cases designed especially to hold specimens. He had decided to make a start with the 12 commonest orders. The others would have to wait a while. Neatly, he ranged the open Schmitt boxes along the length of the work table. Now he went over to where the piles of "unsorted" boxes were gathering dust, lifted down the topmost one and took it over to the work table. Carefully, with a special pin forceps in his hand, he lifted out his first specimen. It was, unmistakably, a grasshopper. Lutz transferred it to the first empty box and labeled it *Orthoptera*. This was the order to which not only grasshoppers belong, but also crickets, cockroaches, mantids, and their kin.

A start had been made. This initial sorting by order would go fairly quickly. It didn't after all, require any specialized knowledge to recognize a bee and put it in the *Hymenoptera* box or to know a horsefly and put it in with the other *Diptera*.

But after that the complications would start. Take a typical case: the case of the common click beetle— that funny creature which, if it happens to fall on its back, flips into the air with a loud click, lands on its

feet (usually), and runs away. A click beetle and all other beetles belong to the order *Coleoptera*. This order is divided into two sub-orders which are, in turn, divided into 102 families. The click belongs to one of these families, the *Elateridae*. But within this family there are no less than 500 different species in North America alone—and hundreds of other species of click in other parts of the world! So sorting out the common click beetle might seem easy at first. Order, sub-order, family. No problem. But then very soon it would involve closer inspection with the magnifying glass, then checking with all sorts of different reference works and specimens already in the identified collections until the specimen in Lutz's forceps might be one of only a dozen species. Then, as the differences between the related species became more and more minute, there would be more microscopic examination, more checking and so on and on and on, until the possible species were narrowed down to eight, five, three. Finally, one small characteristic, impossible to see without the microscope, would definitely place the specimen in one species. Now at last it could be labeled with its full name and sorted into its proper place.

It is hardly surprising that it did take years—three to be exact—for the entomology department to make any real progress with this phase of its work. Meanwhile, Lutz soon found out, there were several other important jobs to be done. There were exhibits to be planned, research projects to be studied, lectures to be given to Museum visitors, pamphlets and papers to be written. . .He had never been so busy.

He had never been so happy, either. He loved his

work at the Museum, with all its varied facets. Even the classifying and sorting, while often tedious, were gratifying to him, as he gradually saw his efforts make order out of chaos.

But there was one thing he didn't like: living in New York City. Used to the freedom of the outdoors he loved, he felt caged in by the city.

A few months of apartment living were all he could stand. No child of his, he told his wife one day, would be brought up in the city. That settled it. Just as soon as possible the Lutz family, which now included two children, moved to the pleasant country town of Ramsey, New Jersey.

Hardly had Mrs. Lutz finished unpacking in their new home when her husband hurried home early one afternoon in high excitement. He was about to accompany Professor Crampton on what would be his first field expedition for the Museum. Their destination would be the wild interior of British Guiana. Their purpose was to get samples of insect life from the forests and savannahs of that region for a South American collection the department was starting.

On a warm afternoon in June the expedition began. First, the two scientists went by ship to the West Indies and then continued south. Days later Lutz saw in the distance what looked like a series of lighthouses jutting out in the sky. They were, he learned later, the smoke stacks of sugar mills surrounding Georgetown, British Guiana. It was his first view of the South American continent.

Then the inland journey began. First by river steamer and then by train they traveled, through miles and miles of sugar cane fields. Gradually the scenery changed. The second day out from George-town, the cultivated cane fields gave way to woods. Then, as the miles went by, the woods grew thicker and thicker until they became dense jungle-like forest. Very slowly the travelers penetrated deeper into the interior—now by river launch, sometimes by foot through steaming jungle, finally by native rowboat.

Once more the scenery changed. From the river-banks on either side of them great tree-covered prec-ipices rose up. Now, a week after their start from Georgetown, they had reached the foothills of the mountain region they were seeking.

Suddenly they turned a bend in the Potaro River. There, glimmering in the distance, was the sight they'd been searching for—the mighty Kaieteur Falls.

It was one of the most magnificent spectacles Frank Lutz was ever to see. From the Guiana Highlands above, the great waters rushed down 800 feet into the river below. Few Americans had ever heard of the Kaieteur Falls, although they were five times higher than those at Niagara! Thrilled by the stupendous sight, Frank Lutz almost forgot that this was the des-tination he had traveled so far to reach.

Kaieteur was the end of the road for him. Pro-fessor Crampton would push ahead into the interior, to the great plateau region on the Brazilian border. But Lutz was to stay behind to explore the forests and savannahs around Kaieteur.

Left with him as helpers were two Indian boys, both about 12 years old. They were from a very primitive tribe—"almost entirely untouched by civilization," Lutz wrote home. But they were happy, friendly boys and anxious to be helpful.

Every day for the next three weeks, Lutz and his helpers roamed the territory for miles around, hunting insects wherever they went. At daybreak they would set out. This was the best time to find lots of light-avoiding insects. Perhaps, he hoped, he would find among them the great *Caligo* or owl butterfly with the strange eye-spot markings on the underside of its wings.

To any natives who were watching, they must have seemed a bizarre trio of hunters, with the unlikely assortment of "weapons" they carried. Always there was one insect net, and often two—a heavy one for sweeping the brush, a lighter one for catching butterflies and other flying creatures. One of his helpers would carry a big black umbrella, to serve as a beating cloth for catching those insects which might be found on trees. In their packs would also be special entomology forceps, a geologist's pick, an axe, and several wooden boxes lined with cotton for storing insects once they had been killed. They also had an assortment of killing jars. Some contained alcohol for "wet collecting"—that is, for soft-bodied creatures like spiders, most insect larvae, and certain adult species. Others were "dry" killing jars, with a layer of plaster of paris that covered crystals of deadly cyanide.

All day long they hunted. Back and forth Lutz would sweep his heavy net as he walked through the tropical forest. In no time at all the net was a mass of life which would then be quickly picked over on the spot, to be sorted out later. Or he might use his lightweight aerial net to capture one of the countless exquisite butterflies or moths that seemed to abound in the forest. Then, having landed a prize, he would very expertly pinch it just under the wings to stun it. This would prevent it from battering itself against the sides of the killing jar (it takes about half an hour in the jar to kill an insect—plenty of time for a panicky butterfly to do itself terrible damage).

Sometimes he would take to "beating"—hitting branches or bushes hard with a stick while insects tumbled off them into the upturned umbrella held by one of the boys below. He and the boys would pry up rocks and turn stones over to uncover the insects hiding under them. He would hack away at tree stumps with his pick and axc, dig into the ground, scrape bark off trees, slide his net up tree tunks or brush it along more delicate plants. Insects were to be found everywhere, in everything.

Back at the camp in the evening the hunt would continue. The night-flying species must be caught too. As darkness closed in, Lutz would set up the trap. It consisted of a gasoline Coleman lantern with a sheet hanging behind it and heavy tarpaulin spread out on the ground underneath. In vast numbers the insects came, sometimes a cloud of them hiding the lantern's light, shattering the night stillness with a tremendous humming of wings and thudding of bodies as they hit the sheet and fell stunned onto the tarpaulin below. Close by Lutz or one of the boys was waiting, ready to pick them up as they fell. Unless he moved quickly, other insects would get there first, destructive ones that would ruin his specimens.

There was other work to be done, too. One vitally important job was preparing and packing the day's catch—usually around 400 specimens. The hard-bodied insects had to be dried out first to prevent decay. Then they were packed very carefully into boxes lined with cotton. Some he would pin then and there. Others, such as butterflies and other large-winged insects, would be placed in special triangular envelopes and still others in paper tubes. And always, for each and every specimen, a label must be written, giving place, date, and time of its capture.

In the evening, too, Lutz would sit by the flickering light of his kerosene lamp, writing detailed notes about the specimens in the day's "catch."

One evening as he sat writing, he noticed one of the boys working busily with a long piece of string. It was the boy he had nicknamed Cricket. He had had to invent names for both boys because they refused to give their real names. To tell the American your name, the natives believed, was to give him power to call down the devil on your fortunes.

Curious, Lutz went over to see what was happening. He was astounded. Here in the middle of a South American jungle, this half-savage young Indian lad was playing exactly the same "cat's cradle" tricks as his own children back in New Jersey played. He watched, fascinated. Cricket was a real artist with the string. He was making patterns now that were much more elaborate than any Lutz had ever seen before. He wanted to learn some of these to show his children. So in the weeks that followed, after the day's work was over, Frank Lutz, the learned entomologist, would take his seat beside Cricket, the primitive young Indian, to be taught the mysteries of these highly complicated versions of cat's cradle.

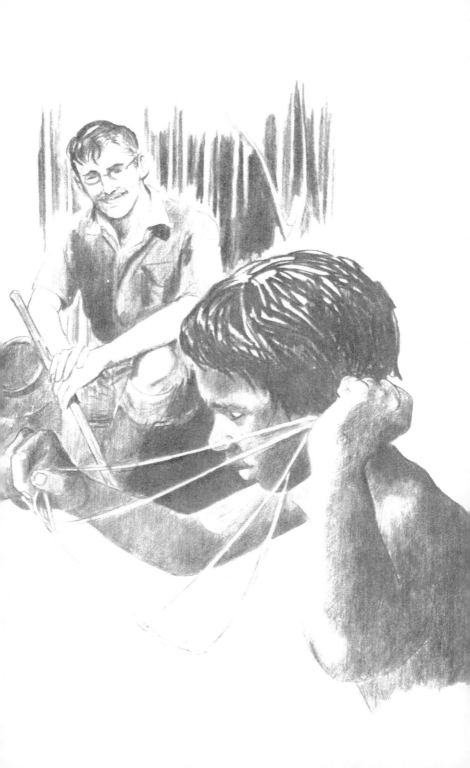

Seldom, in those three weeks, did a day last any less than 18 hours. Yet never before had the hours flown so quickly. For this field trip was the most exciting adventure of his life.

He was sure that nothing could equal the tropics for color, for fascination, for sheer abundance of life. Nowhere else in the world was nature so full of such striking contrasts. This was the home of the brilliant morpho, among the most spectacular creatures on earth. In these same forests flitted that fragile ghostly beauty, the glass wing butterfly, which the Indians believe to be the soul of a departed child. This was the region of giant, larger-than-life insects: grasshoppers over four inches long; rhinoceros beetles 20 times bigger than their North American cousins; fat cockroaches the size of a small mouse. But it was also the home of tiny creatures: minute wasps, much smaller than any of our species; delicate *Agrion* dragonflies; miniature moths, little jewels of perfection.

At the end of three weeks Professor Crampton returned to Kaieteur from Brazil, and the long journey home began. Lutz's first field expedition had been a tremendous experience for him, and a fruitful one for the Museum. Between them, Lutz and Crampton had caught more than 30,000 specimens. The Museum's new South American collection was off to an excellent start. And, thanks to Cricket's lessons, Lutz's children would have interesting new games to play. He had another odd souvenir: a present for his children from Cricket. He called it Cricket's best suit. It consisted of one brightly colored handmade belt—the only article of clothing Cricket ever wore.

4

Insects See the Light

Dr. Frank Lutz got up from his desk and stretched. He had spent that whole Saturday at home working on his first book. He had started writing it a year or two ago, and it was still not quite completed. It was to be a guide to the insects of the United States. Nothing quite like it had ever been done before. After several years of sorting out the Museum's collections, identifying thousands after thousands of tiny creatures, he was one of the best qualified men in the country to write a book of this sort. After all, he was a curator of the largest insect collection in the United States. His book would help people identify for themselves the flying and crawling things they found in every part of the country. It would tell them about the wonderful transformations that take place in each insect's life, that some insects can be harmful to man, but that most are harmless and even necessary to Nature's scheme of things.

He had known when he started on it that it would take him several years, writing after his work at the Museum, to complete the *Field Book of Insects*. But he hoped to produce a volume so definitive that it would become a standard reference guide for generations of students as well as the curious. (He succeeded. Published originally in 1918, and revised twice since then, it is still considered an essential part of the libraries of professional and amateur entomologists alike.)

Right now he needed a change after so many hours of writing. He started toward the door to join his children (there were four of them now, three girls and a boy) and their friends, playing in the yard. He had enviously heard their fun all afternoon. But on his way his eyes fell on a book he had just brought home from the Museum library. It was *Ants, Bees and Wasps,* by Sir John Lubbock, an Englishman who had lived during the 1800's and had been not only a famous statesman and banker but also a brilliant entomologist. He would just pick up the book for a minute before going out to enjoy the sun and the fun.

He started leafing through its pages. As he flipped, a few lines on one page caught his eye. He turned back to read the paragraph more carefully. The words leaped up at him:

"These experiments seem to me very interesting. They appear to prove that ants perceive the ultraviolet rays."

His attention riveted now on this new idea, he forgot completely about the children and games in the yard. Quickly he turned back to the start of the section.

Lubbock was describing an experiment he had made with ants. It had been observed that worker ants, when their nest is disturbed, frantically rush to carry their larvae and pupae from the light into the darkest place they can find. Lubbock had set up a situation that would test the ants' reactions to light and color. He placed a group of adult ants and pupae in a long narrow box, and arranged the lighting so that it would produce an entire spectrum, ranging from red at one end through orange, yellow, green, blue, violet, and, at the other end, even ultraviolet. To his surprise, as soon as they were placed in the box, the adults had snatched up the pupae from the ultraviolet section and scampered off to deposit them in the red-colored areas. Clearly ultraviolet, a color so dark to us we cannot see it, looked bright to these ants. And red, to us a bright color, appeared dark to them.

Lutz was fascinated. If ants could see color and light in a way that humans couldn't, how about other insects? Sometime he must explore this intriguing problem. But right now, between his work at the Museum and his book, he had his hands more than full. Anyway, it was still a lovely day out and the children still waited in the yard.

Months passed. Then one afternoon, a physicist friend, Dr. Floyd K. Richtmyer, a professor at Cornell University, visited him in Ramsey. Richtmyer was internationally known for his work with X-rays and scientific photography. Lutz thought his visitor might be interested in Lubbock's experiment. As he described it, Richtmyer listened with growing interest.

Lutz continued, saying it would be a good idea to

confirm Lubbock's results by making some more tests, but that he himself was too busy now for the elaborate series of experiments that would be necessary. But, the physicist suggested, surely they could do just a quick test now.

Lutz didn't need much persuading. So they ran off a test to see if *Drosophila* could see ultraviolet. They decided to cover a glass tube with paper and expose one end of it to ultraviolet light, using a glass filter that would cut off all the visible rays being produced by a special ultraviolet generator. Would the little flies go toward that end of the tube, and thereby prove that they were sensitive to ultraviolet? Very definitely they did.

Now Lutz's curiosity was really aroused. What other insects might have ultraviolet vision, he wondered. What about bees and wasps and butterflies and all those other flower-visiting insects so vital to the fertilization of flowers? It had always been taken for granted that they see colors the same as humans do, and that it was the colors of the flowers, as much as the odors, that attracted them. Maybe this was not so after all. It would be well worth trying to find out.

He had finally finished work on the book, and so he could devote himself to this new challenge. He set to work preparing the test he wanted to make. A more complicated apparatus than the simple tube he and Richtmyer had used would be needed. He constructed a long narrow box with an opening at each end into which could be fitted little glass windows of different colors. The family yard would be his laboratory. One Saturday morning he carried the box out into the yard for the first test. The experiment was about to begin.

First he set the box up with a window that filtered out everything but ultraviolet light. The glass was so dark and dense he couldn't read print through it, because it did not transmit any of the colors to which human eyes are sensitive. At the other end of the box, he put in a piece of transparent orange-colored glass. The top of the box was clear glass but he put a black cloth hood over it, big enough to cover his head so he could watch every move his insects made without letting in any daylight.

Now, with the help of his son Frank, he went on a hunt for flower-visiting insects. It was easy work. The sun was out, it was a glorious warm day, and the yard was bright with flowers in bloom. Soon they had an excellent assortment of insects in their jars.

Now very carefully, Lutz transferred his first subject—a honeybee worker—into the box. Young Frank had put his head inside the hood to have the first look. For perhaps half a minute there was silence. Then Frank let out a muffled cheer from inside the hood. The bee had headed straight for the ultraviolet window.

This was what they had hoped would happen. But they still had a long way to go. It was time for the next stage. With the bee still buzzing around the ultraviolet window, Lutz very cautiously exchanged it for a dark, muddy brown window. Then he replaced the orange window at the other end with a piece of clear glass. He watched for the bee's reaction. Again he switched windows, then a third time, then a fourth. A total of ten times in all, he tried out different color combinations on the bee.

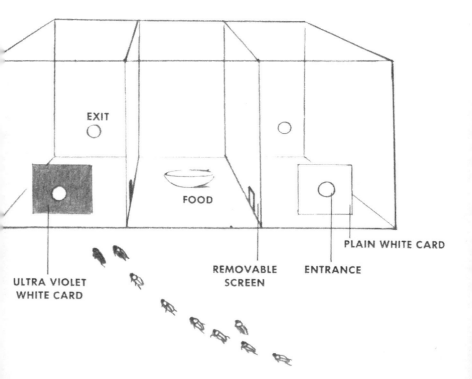

EXIT

ULTRA VIOLET
WHITE CARD

FOOD

REMOVABLE
SCREEN

ENTRANCE

PLAIN WHITE CARD

It was the same story every time: if one of the windows was ultraviolet, the bee headed straight for it.

After the tenth test, he set the bee free. It had been a perfect subject—reacted throughout exactly as he had hoped. For in setting up the experiment he had reasoned that an insect, trying to get out of the box, would make for the opening that looked brightest to it. Quite obviously, to this bee at least, ultraviolet looked the brightest of all the colors he had used.

He was off to a good start. Now he selected his second subject—a silver spotted skipper butterfly. But it proved very uncooperative, sometimes even refusing to budge at all until it was tapped lightly or the box shaken. Still Lutz went through the entire experiment from start to finish, changing windows ten different times and painstakingly noting each time the slightest movement of the butterfly, the slightest reaction to each change. It was a long-drawn-out, tedious affair. But, even if slowly, the skipper seemed to respond in the same way as the bee: if one of the windows was ultraviolet, it sooner or later fluttered to that one.

Next Lutz put in a syrphid fly. Unlike the butterfly it reacted promptly to each change of windows, passing all the tests with flying colors. Then a bumblebee followed. After that he tried a wasp, then a tiger swallowtail butterfly, then a ladybird beetle, then a solitary bee, then a rove beetle, then an angel-wing butterfly, then many, many more. Day after day, weekend after weekend he spent out in the yard, bent over his box, head inside the hood. One after another the insects were put through the series of tests while he very carefully noted the very slightest reaction of each.

Finally one evening he carried the box inside the house. He would need it no more. Test after test after test had supplied him with more than enough data.

"Two things seem to be quite certain," he reported. "The first is that, whether insects perceive red, green, yellow, blue and ultraviolet as colors or merely as illumination, they are affected by and react to each of these, including red and ultraviolet. The second is that the insects see ultraviolet as a strong light; in other words, they see it well—even better than other light."

He had, in short, discovered that when it came to color, the vision of insects is quite different from human vision.

Highly excited, he communicated his findings to Dr. Richtmyer at once. Next, he said, he wanted to find out if there might be ultraviolet-colored flowers —just as there are red-colored, orange, and blue flowers. Would Richtmyer be interested in exploring the matter?

Richtmyer was most interested. It just happened he had started doing a little work on insect-flower relations.

First, however, preparations had to be made. This would be a much more complicated experiment than the previous one. As the physicist and expert in spectrography, it was Richtmyer's job to devise the procedure they would use. Using special photographic and spectrographic equipment they would be able to discover all the colors a given flower reflected—even those colors that the human eye cannot see, such as ultraviolet. They would also be able to measure precisely how much ultraviolet there was.

First to have their "portraits" taken were some portulacas in the Lutz yard. A few days later Richtmyer called Lutz. He had just finished processing the spectrographs and now had his first results: all the portulacas were strongly ultraviolet.

This was completely unexpected! The two scientists had purposely selected three flowers of different colors. They had photographed red, yellow and pink portulacas. Yet to an insect all three would appear exactly the same color: ultraviolet.

What, they wondered, about other flowers? How did the rest of the garden look to an insect?

All summer Lutz and Richtmyer spent taking their special photographs of countless different flowers. They got a wide variety of results. Some, like the portulacas, were strongly ultraviolet. Others, such as zinnias, reflected no ultraviolet at all. And others still had striking ultraviolet patterns—black-eyed Susans were an example of these. Their yellow petals were ultraviolet only at the tip, not at the base. What a very different view insects must have of flowers!

At the summer's end Lutz and Richtmyer made public their findings. They created quite a stir in biological circles, for they had shattered a long-held notion: namely, that floral colors appear the same to other creatures as to humans. Color had long been considered a very important factor in insect-flower relations. It had been generally believed, as Lutz put it, "that a particular flower has its particular color because that color is the one best adapted to getting insects to come to it."

Between them, Lutz and Richtmyer had definitely shown that belief to be wrong. But could ultraviolet, perhaps, be the key? In discovering ultraviolet in flowers, had they discovered a hitherto unknown key attraction for insects? It was a question that had to be answered.

The most obvious approach was to find out if insects visited ultraviolet flowers more than other flowers. To do this, Lutz conducted a series of five- and ten-minute observations of a group of different flowers. The results were not dramatic, and he concluded that "ultraviolet flowers are, other things being as equal as possible, no more popular with insects than are flowers reflecting only the colors that are visible to man."

He decided to try something else. He had read of bees being trained to come to certain colors for food. How would they respond to ultraviolet? That is what he wanted to find out.

By way of equipment he made some boxes, each of which had three compartments separated from each other by removable wire screens. In the center compartment he placed some sweetened water for food; the two side sections served as passageways into the food chamber. Bees could easily get into the two end rooms—both had entrances from the outside. But he could stop them from getting to the food chamber by blocking it off at either end with the wire screens.

At the entrances to the two end rooms he put two seemingly identical white cards. One, however, strongly reflected ultraviolet, the other did not. From the ultraviolet entrance the bees could go directly to the food. But if they used the plain white entrance, they would find the passage to the food room blocked.

Now he set out the boxes in the yard and waited for the field bees to approach. He sat, waiting and watching. At first nothing much happened. Then, very, very gradually, things started to change. First a few of the bolder bees ventured inside the boxes. Then the traffic at both entrances increased. Now, very slightly at first, another change took place: little by little, fewer and fewer bees went to the plain white entrance. Finally, they deserted it completely. All were now using the ultraviolet entrance.

They had given him all the proof he needed. Certainly they had gone to the ultraviolet door. But they had also, at the start, gone to the plain white one. Obviously ultraviolet in itself held no magnetic attraction for them. But they had come to realize—and in a very short time—that it meant food. That was the only reason they had gone to the ultraviolet.

One day late that summer, shortly after he had reached these conclusions, some friends of the Lutz family came to visit. With his bee-testing apparatus still set up in the yard, Frank Lutz could not resist playing a practical joke on his guests. He informed them that he had taught the bees to read. "As a matter of fact," he said, "I have succeeded in making spelling bees."

Curious, his friends insisted, "Show us."

"All right," said the entomologist. He went into the house and returned to the yard with a pencil and two white cards.

"I'm going to put this card at the right side of the box, here, next to the door that does not lead to the food," he explained, as he handed the card and the pencil to one of his friends. "Write anything you want on it, but be sure to use the word 'not.'"

The friend thought for a minute, then wrote "Food is not here."

"Fine," said Frank Lutz, taking the card and putting it in its place. "Now write anything you want to on this other card, but be sure to use the word 'yes.'"

His friend took the second card, and wrote "Yes, this is the way to food."

Dr. Lutz placed the second card near the other door of the box, and told his friends to wait patiently. In a few minutes, he promised, his "spelling bees" would arrive.

They did. A few of them did wander into the "not" door, but after only a moment's hesitation almost all of them made the proverbial bee-line for the "yes" entrance. His friends were amazed, and watched the performance, mystified, for the rest of the afternoon.

In the interests of science, he divulged the secret of the ultraviolet card just before they went home.

5

The Stingless Bees of Panama

"I am a museum curator," Dr. Lutz told the group of visitors, "and museum men are supposed by some to spend their lives collecting and naming things. If that were my only work in connection with the Museum, I would resign."

After more than a dozen years in the turreted palace on Central Park West, he was still fascinated with his job. The public seemed to have the odd notion that museums, and people who work in them, were dull and dusty. Well, he had to admit that some dust could be found on the stacks of books and storage cases in his laboratory. But his life and his place of work were far from dull. In fact, he was sure, things must be much duller for salesmen, or housewives, or even actuaries. He was glad he had been spared. For him, life was exciting indeed.

He had the excitement of correctly identifying specimens, the pleasure of instructing visitors, the thrill of seeing children view an insect with new appreciation after he told them of its life. He enjoyed discussing advances in the sciences with a varied group of colleagues. He was intrigued by the gaps in man's understanding of the animal world, and he constantly devised and carried out experiments in an attempt to lessen those gaps and increase that understanding.

Of all his varied activities, the ones that excited him most were the field trips. The public, he was sure, didn't know about that aspect of museum work at all. Yet he himself had gone on a field trip almost every year since joining the Museum. Sometimes they were collecting expeditions, but very often they were primarily for studying insect behavior. So far, his trips had taken him to the tropical forests of South America, the swamps of Cuba, the deserts of Arizona, the snowy peaks of Colorado and Wyoming, and the wild Everglades of Florida. He had just returned from one of the most unusual ones, to Gatun Lake in Panama.

That adventure had started the year before, when a man who had lived in the tropics for many years presented a superb collection of *Trigona* to the Museum. *Trigona* are a genus of honeybee found only in the tropics. They are very small, no more than a quarter of an inch long. Also they do not sting.

Studying the collection, Lutz was intrigued by the marked differences between the various species of the stingless bees. Now he wanted to obtain more specimens of adults for the Museum, as well as the nests and young of as many species as he could find.

His destination was Barro Colorado, an island in Gatun Lake in the Canal Zone. Only a few years earlier, the island had been a mountaintop overlooking the Chagres River valley. During construction of the Panama Canal, the river was dammed up, an artificial lake was created, and the mountain was submerged. Just before Lutz's visit in 1923, Barro Colorado had been set aside by the U.S. Government as a wildlife preserve, the only one in a tropical territory of the United States. Lutz was very curious to look over its insect population in general, and to study several species of *Trigona* in particular.

Ancon, in the Canal Zone, was his first stop. He set out to see the sights carrying, as usual, an insect net. This one was a pocket version, since he did not want to be too conspicuous in a strange place. Even in cities, he claimed, you could find interesting insects.

He was right. Hardly had he stepped outside his hotel than, right in front of him, a red-bellied *Trigona* flew up from the edge of the pavement. A second followed, then a third. He looked. Right here, in the heart of a city, underneath a cement sidewalk, these little creatures had built themselves a nest.

Lutz was in a dilemma. On the one hand, he was longing to get down and examine his first *Trigona* nest. But on the other hand, he was rather embarrassed. After all, it was his first day in the country. The streets were crowded with passersby. "And," he reflected, "it really is not quite the thing for a dignified American to be seen on his hands and knees on the pavement. People might not understand!"

Reluctantly, he decided to pass it by. He consoled

himself with the realization that, where he was going, he would have lots of opportunities to examine *Trigona* nests.

The next day he set off by railroad on the second stage of the trip. The train chugged along noisily, on one side of it a green barrier of forest, on the other the long stretches of the Panama Canal. It was a peaceful, pleasant scene. Yet only 20 years before this very place had been called "the foremost pest-hole" of the earth, "infamous for its fevers and interesting only because of the variety of its malarial disorders and pestilences."

Two tiny creatures had earned the country its terrible reputation: the *Aëdes aegypti* mosquito, carrier of yellow fever, and the *Anopheles* mosquito, carrier of malaria. Despite their size they had, between them, formed the biggest single obstacle to the Building of the Panama Canal—more critical by far than any problems of engineering or construction. Only when the dread scourge of disease was lifted, through the mosquito-control programs of General Gorgas, could the workers construct the Canal.

At the train's next stop, Lutz got off and made final preparations for the trip to Barro Colorado: he bought a native canoe and hired a native helper named Murillo.

At sunrise the following morning they set off in their canoe and after two hours of paddling reached the island: 12 square miles of uninhabited jungle that would be their home and laboratory for the next two weeks. In what was left of a rough shack, Lutz pitched his tent. Then he ventured out to explore.

He had never seen anything like it! This tropical jungle was fantastic in a way that was difficult to explain. Part of its fascination lay in the dense tangles of trees and vines, in the constant gloom and dampness, in the chattering monkeys, the spectacular birds.

"But jungle is more than all of these," Lutz wrote later, "It is *jungle*, indescribable, fascinating and, to the biologist, an environment of extreme interest."

It was also impenetrable. Before they could work, Murillo, an expert with the machete, had to cut a trail across the island. As he swung his machete, Lutz followed, swinging his insect net.

The jungle was teeming with insects; raucous Panama cicadas; bizarre leafhoppers with weird "horns" on their backs; tropical cockroaches three inches long; brilliant butterflies; beetles and bugs of all shapes and sizes; that fantastic native of the tropics, the stalk-eyed fly, with eyes that quite literally jut out on long stalks on either side of its head; bees and wasps and hornets; termites; and, above all, ants: a group of fierce azteca ants attacking an intruder; lines of leafcutting ants bobbing along with their burdens of leaf which they use to fertilize the kind of mushroom they grow for food; and that most terrifying of insects, the blind carnivorous army-ant. When on the march, their armies of 10,000 to 100,000 strong devour every living creature in their path. Even an animal the size of a horse, if tethered and unable to escape, could be reduced to a skeleton in a matter of a few hours by these relentless creatures.

Then Lutz saw a wasp nest and, with Murillo looking on terror-stricken, proceeded to take it. Very cautiously he moved, yet at the same time, very smoothly to make sure the wasps wouldn't be alarmed by jerky movements. It was all over and done with—and not one sting. Murillo looked at Lutz speechless with wonder.

That night, after Lutz and Murillo had gone to bed, the native called to his employer. Could he, please, ask a favor? And if Lutz would grant it, he, Murillo, would work for him without further pay.

"What is it you want?" asked the scientist, who had an idea what was coming.

"Please, sir, some of the medicine you use. So you don't get hurt with the wasp nest."

Hiding his amusement, and taking the opportunity to explain a basic fact of insect behavior, Lutz explained carefully. "Wild things are not dangerous when you act properly toward them. My only medicine was common sense. I moved slowly, calmly, but without pausing. I knew what I had to do, and I did not hesitate. I was not afraid, and I did not make the wasps afraid. I did not frighten them, and they did not sting me."

The next morning he showed Murillo what he meant, but he came to the conclusion that the Panamanian would never learn how. It took practice, but in part it also depended upon an inborn gift. Some people never got the knack. Murillo, Lutz suspected, was probably one of them.

He had no trouble catching the stingless bees he had come for. They were constant visitors at the shack, where they sampled all of his food supplies. Unlike the Northern honeybee, which limits its diet to pollen

and nectar, the *Trigona* were regular scavengers.

"They are not very choice in their diet," Lutz wrote in his journal. "Not only did they raid everything in our larder but the garbage cans in Panama City were also popular and I have caught such bees on manure and dead snakes."

As an afterthought he added, "I am not very anxious to try their honey."

He was surprised by their odd nesting habits. He had read that they nested in hollow tree stumps. Accordingly, he and Murillo set off to search the jungle for hollow stumps. Just a little way along their trail Lutz stopped suddenly. A fine termites' nest had caught his eye. It looked to be three feet across, jutting out like some great swelling on the trunk of a tree. Around an opening at the top hovered a number of tiny bees. He went over to inspect. They had built themselves a nest inside the termites' nest. What's more, the termites were still there, too! They were in the lower part, the *Trigona* in the upper section—and the two colonies seemed to be living side by side in utter peace and harmony.

This was no unique experience, he was to find. In the days ahead, he came across several more *Trigona* nests in termites' nests. He also found them occupying a deserted ants' nest. He even found a few nests where he expected to: in hollow tree stumps.

The nests themselves were extraordinary. At the top of each was a clay funnel—this was the entrance. Where the domestic honeybee uses only wax and resin for building materials, these untidy little creatures seemed to use anything and everything. Later, he examined the inside of one. It was cluttered with bits of gum, resin, plant fuzz, clay, wax, manure, all sorts of strange things. It was a real garbage heap.

All too soon Lutz's 10 days on his jungle island were up. He had got what he had come for: about 2,000 assorted insects; specimens of several different species of *Trigona* and, best of all, six fine specimens of *Trigona* nests. But almost all his time had been spent collecting. Next time, he would like to spend more time observing the habits of the fauna of this fascinating place.

Trigona had yet another surprise in store for him. On his way back to Panama City, while waiting for a car, he noticed many of them flying in and out of a brush pile. Curious, he went over to study the brush pile more closely. A rambling Solanum plant, related to the potato and tomato, was growing there. Feeding on the solanum was a colony of immature tree hoppers, and the scavenger *Trigona*, in turn, were feeding on their secretions.

This was amazing. There were, he knew, lots of insect "partnerships." To scientists, this interrelation of different species is known as *symbiosis*. One of the best known involves ants and aphids (pests, commonly known as plant lice). The ants actually tend colonies of aphids to lick up the "honeydew" that comes from the. Often, if the aphids aren't supplying enough honeydew the ants "milk" them by stroking them with their antennae. The ants may even build shelters of mud to protect their herds of "ants' cows," as aphids are sometimes called.

But this little scene between *Trigona* and the treehoppers was something he had never witnessed before. It would, he thought, be a perfect finishing touch to the paper he would write about the tropical bee when he returned.

6
Bringing Insect Life to the Public

Before he knew it he was back at the Museum, working on his *Trigona* collection, writing the report on his field trip, supervising his department, and still addressing groups of visitors.

Some of the other curators thought this part of their work to be a chore, a waste of time that could better be spent on research. But not Frank Lutz. It was one of his great hopes to get people to learn the truth about insects. Then they would not only find them fascinating to observe, but would also come to appreciate insects for the great good they do.

As Lutz knew only too well, most people react instinctively to an insect by stepping on it. A best-selling item that year was a new kind of insect trap which electrocuted all the creatures that came to it. This kind of thoughtless killing made Lutz angry.

"The wholesale slaughter of insects does much

more harm than good," he would tell people. "It is as bad as releasing poison gas in a crowded restaurant to kill one hold-up man."

He never tired of pointing out that only a fraction of one per cent of the world's huge insect population was in any way destructive or harmful to man. He did not minimize the damage that this fraction could do. Those few species had managed, between them, to kill more people than all the wars in the history of mankind! In his gallery talks he listed the culprits.

Best known were the mosquitoes. But of more than 2,000 species of mosquito, only a few bite. And of these few species, only the adult female does the biting. And of those that bite, only a small percentage are harmful; the rest, merely annoying. But one species alone, the *Anopheles*, carrier of malaria, was responsible for plaguing a large part of the human race. It was another, the *Aëdes aegypti* mosquito, carrier of yellow fever, that had to be eliminated from Panama before the Canal could be built; it had ravaged not only the tropics but, until the early 1900's, large areas of the United States as well. And two other horrible tropical diseases, the deforming elephantiasis and the debilitating dengue fever, were transmitted by still other mosquito species.

Lutz also spoke of other well-known insect pests. *Musca domestica*, the common housefly, was well known to all of his listeners as a symbol of filth and a potential agent for spreading typhoid, dysentery, and a host of other diseases. He would mention lice, unpleasant little creatures that infest the hair and clothing of humans, and the coats of some animals. Lice

79

could be more than annoying, for they could carry typhus, a terrible epidemic disease that still raged through cities of the Middle East and Asia, leaving great numbers of dead in its wake.

He would mention the most vicious insect pest of all, the tiny rat flea, carrier of the dread bubonic plague which spread as rapidly as a fire, engulfing whole cities and nations. Few of its victims ever recovered. The Black Death it had been called in the Middle Ages when it swept throughout all Europe, killing one-quarter of the continent's population, a total of 25,000,000 people. As recently as the early 1900's the bubonic plague had raged throughout India, leaving six million dead. If not for the rigid safety measures taken immediately by other countries, the plague might have spread throughout the world.

He would list other troublemakers: the tsetse fly of Africa, carrier of sleeping sickness; some tropical assassin bugs that spread the rare but terrible Chagas' disease; even certain kinds of cockroach that have been blamed for spreading disease. (A thoroughly disagreeable creature, the cockroach, but one deserving some respect, he would tell the visitors, as one of the most ancient of all living creatures—dating right back to the Coal Age some 320 million years ago!)

Then he would mention another long list of insects which, though not killers, could still cause acute pain: the *Culex* mosquito, the horsefly, the bee, the wasp, certain ants, the black fly, certain caterpillars, the incredibly hardy bedbug. He had just read of a bedbug that survived an entire year of being kept in a container without any food at all.

Yet, though a few species are destructive, most insects are tremendously beneficial to mankind. And this was what he was leading up to. They make possible most of the vegetables we eat, as well as most of the fruits; the cotton, silk, and linen we wear; the flowers in our yards; the tobacco some people smoke —the list goes on and on. "We would not have any orchards," he would explain, "if it were not for the insects that carry pollen from flower to flower. Some insects may destroy, say, twenty per cent of our fruit crops. But other insects make possible the eighty per cent that we harvest."

He would explain that Nature supplies definite controls to keep a balance between different forms of life and prevent any one species from getting too far out of hand. One of Nature's best controls against insects is other insects. Probably the best known example is the ladybird beetle, which befriends us by killing such pests as the aphid and scale insect. But there are thousands of other insect friends: caterpillar hunters and other carabid beetles, mantises, syrphid maggots, pentatomid bugs—and that cunning trapper, the ant lion larva, which digs pits into the sand and then waits in ambush for an unsuspecting ant or other insect to tumble into the trap!

Lutz recommended our use of natural controls such as these whenever possible. He warned against man-made interference. "When Man interferes with Nature's biological set-up, he is very apt to make a mess of it," he observed.

(These words, spoken several decades ago, have a prophetic ring. From the early 1940's on—just about

81

the time of Lutz's death—chemical controls began to be used in significant amounts. Insecticides and pesticides, hailed as the solution to insect damage, flooded the market and covered the fields. But recently man is having second thoughts, as it is being realized that not just our insect pests but also our insect allies, our plant life, our fish, birds, and other living creatures may be harmed in the process. Today there is a trend toward the natural controls that Lutz advocated so long ago.)

Then he would try to convey some of the fascination that the insect world held for him.

"They keep 'cows,' " he said, "building sheds to cover them. They make gardens; have slaves; build houses for themselves and offspring; they dig caves; hollow out wood; sing songs; catch prey and have all sorts of devices to keep from being caught; they go to live with their relatives and make themselves generally interesting."

After he had finished talking, he would steer the group over to the Insect Hall, to explore on their own. Sometimes he would follow after them, looking at the exhibits with a critical eye. Were the displays doing the best possible job of telling their story?

He was now, among other jobs, in charge of all exhibits there, having been made head of the department two years ago, in 1921. Some of the exhibits certainly were striking. But large areas of the gallery looked like a kind of Noah's ark: row upon row of insects neatly pinned two by two, male and female. It was a fabulous mine of information for the student. But how could all these rows of dead insects have any interest for the average museumgoer? What could the "man in the street" gain from them?

What the Hall needed was life. Real life. Live insects. Why not?

He set to work at once, designing and building an insect "zoo." Within a week it was ready. In a glass display case was a dish of drug-store beetles (annoying creatures that will eat their way through all kinds of drug-store supplies—even poisons); several green praying mantises; two tiger-moth larvae; and some water insects, including three of the fierce three-inch giant water-bugs that are known to attack fish more than twice their size!

It really livened up the Insect Hall. But he could see that there was still room for more changes. Why not try something like the exhibits done by certain of the other departments? Some of these were so realistic they looked as though they had come to life. The animals looked so real they seemed to be breathing and the plant life around them so natural it seemed to be growing. He thought about the matter a great deal, met with colleagues, discussed possibilities, exchanged ideas, and drew up plans by the dozen.

This "habitat group" idea had never before been properly tried with insects. It might not work. But there was only one way to find out: make a first model as a test.

Work began immediately. Artists were called in, along with sculptors, other skilled specialists from the department of preparation, and, of course, entomologists. For some three months, the insect department was in a constant upheaval.

Finally, the test exhibit was ready for its unveiling. As the small group of guests caught their first sight of the model, they broke into applause. It was just like looking out onto a meadow on a beautiful summer day. It was as pretty as a painting. Yet at the same time it told something: for it depicted, much more vividly than words ever could, the life history and habits of the Baltimore butterfly.

It was such a triumph, this new exhibit, that right away a second one was started. Then, in time, a third followed, then a fourth; finally there were six in all. One showed a swarm of ladybird beetles (one of man's best friends in the insect world) emerging from their winter quarters on a Colorado mountaintop; another showed the life history of that pretty but unpopular immigrant, the European cabbage butterfly; a fourth was of a frightful army of Japanese beetles totally destroying a peach tree; a fifth was devoted to the tiger swallowtail butterfly; and the sixth showed a group of monarchs, those beautiful butterflies that gather in great flocks each fall to fly southward for the winter.

Each exhibit, however, involved so much delicate, painstaking work that not until 1925 were all six completed. By then Frank Lutz was in the middle of one of the most important, exciting experiments of his career: the creation of the nation's first nature trail, the first completely out-of-doors museum.

It had started the year before when the Museum had set up a small research station in a state park 40 miles from New York City. Here scientists could study insects outdoors, in their natural environment.

One August morning Lutz, who had been working at the research station, drove over to a Boy Scout Camp in nearby Palisades Interstate Park. Young Frank was a camper there, and Lutz had been invited over to talk to the boys and show them a film on insect life his department had just completed. As soon as he arrived he was whisked off to examine some new items in what was one of the camp's proudest showpieces: its nature museum. This was a cabin filled with all kinds of flowers, tree twigs, insects, and snakes. All of these things had been found in the area by the young Scouts and brought in to be labeled and displayed. He had seen it several times that summer, and he was always impressed by the nature museum idea and the constantly growing collection. It was a splendid way, he thought, of making city youngsters aware of the wonders of nature.

That evening as he drove back to the station in the Harriman State Park, he thought again about the boys' little museum. There was such a need for this kind of thing. So many of the city children in the camps around the area only saw the country for a week or two each year.

The camp nature museum was a wonderful idea. But it would be even better to be able to see all the wild things of nature out where they belonged, instead of neatly stacked in a room. If only they could be left where they are, he thought, if only they could be seen alive, they would be so much more interesting to young people.

It must be completely impractical, he decided. After all, nobody had done it yet. Yet gradually, as he kept thinking about it, and talking it over with friends and colleagues, an idea developed. Why not a completely new kind of museum? It would be entirely out-of-doors. Its only exhibits would be those Nature herself provided. But just as a museum labels things for visitors, so this new museum would label its living exhibits.

As early as possible in the summer of 1925 the Lutz family moved up to the Station for the Study of Insects in Harriman State Park. It was an ideal spot for his experiment—near a lot of camps and near New York City.

In the weeks that followed, the peaceful woodlands of the park became a bustling hive of activity. A constant stream of friends and colleagues arrived to give a helping hand. Paths had to be cut and other areas cleared; specimens had to be checked and books consulted; plants had to be identified and lots of labels carefully printed and mounted; special cages had to be made and insects caught—and all as quickly as possible.

By early July they were ready for the first test. Invitations were sent out to all the nature counselors and consultants from the different camps in the area to come to a picnic at the Station.

As the first bus-load arrived, everybody at the Station rushed forward to greet the passengers. They had all worked so hard the last few weeks and were tremendously enthusiastic about the whole project. What would the verdict be?

First, Lutz gave a short talk on what had been done and why. Then the guests were taken over to a spot

in the woods to see the project for themselves. On a tree was a sign:

"A friend somewhat versed in Natural History is taking a walk with you and calling your attention to interesting things."

From this point a narrow path wound its way for a half-mile through woods, past a spring, and by a murmuring brook. Here and there labels pointed out certain of the trees, shrubs, ferns, flowers, and other plants along the path. They didn't just name names, however. They also gave all sorts of interesting facts and information about the different plants. Also along the trail, in special containers, were some of the insects a person might come across on a walk through the woods. There were an "insect orchestra" of cicadas; some walking sticks; various butterflies including the splendid monarch and its extraordinary look-alike, the viceroy; a group of insects that might be found in damp places near a spring; some buffalo treehoppers; and an assortment of aquatic insects that would inhabit the brook.

Farther along was another path, also narrow and about a half mile in length. Here, too, there were labels on different things. Only, instead of giving facts, these asked questions to find out how much the visitor might know about what he had seen. This was called the Testing Trail. The first path was the Training Trail.

It was really very simple. So simple, indeed, that the guests looked at each other with amazement. Why *had* nobody ever thought of this before?

The counselors could hardly wait to get back to

their own camps to start Nature Trails of their own. Within a few weeks, no less than 20 different Nature Trails had been created in camps around the area.

The idea spread like wildfire. All over the United States, in camps and parks and woods, Nature Trails sprang up. Within a year the idea crossed oceans, too, and trails appeared even as far away as China!

As for the first Nature Trail, it was overrun with visitors all summer long.

Lutz was taken completely by surprise. He had thought of the project as another experiment, another new type of museum exhibit. An experiment in outdoor education, he called it. And it had been a wonderfully exciting experience for those who worked with him. "We had all the fun of invention, all the joy of discovery," he said. He had hoped that the trail would attract children from the camps around and that they would enjoy their visits. But he hadn't expected much more. He had certainly never imagined starting a nationwide trend.

He would be even more astonished today. For in that very same Harriman State Park there are right at this moment not one but several Nature Trails, where the first one was started by Frank Lutz 40 years ago.

7
A Lot of Insects

One day Lutz went to the office of Dr. Frederic A. Lucas, then director of the American Museum of Natural History. The entomology department was very shorthanded, and Lutz had planned an urgent appeal for more staff members. It was not the first time he had argued this particular case, but somehow the Museum's budget had not been able to stretch enough to meet his demands. Well, he would keep trying.

By now Lutz had many eloquent arguments to support his request: the amount of work to be done on the insect collection; how overworked his present staff was; how they could improve their services to the public. He would also bring up how much research was yet to be done in entomology, a science he was fond of describing as "still in its infancy."

This is still the case. New species are even today

being discovered and identified at the rate of about 6,000 a year. Right now, the number of known species stands at about 800,000. When all the species in the world have been discovered, entomologists estimate that there may be as many as two million different species in all! A recent census of the United States insect population has placed the number of species in this country at 83,000.

Statistics like these gave Lutz what he thought was his most persuasive argument. "Taking into consideration only those species known right now," he said to Dr. Lucas, "there are more than three times as many species of insects as there are of *all other kinds* of animals put together! By rights, three-fourths of the employees of any zoological museum should be in the entomology department!"

Dr. Lucas smiled, and admitted that the Museum's insects did need more caretakers.

Warming to his subject, Lutz continued, "Why, more different kinds of insects either live in or come to my modest back yard, in the middle of a suburban town, than there are different kinds of birds in all of the United States and Canada."

"Surely you are exaggerating," replied the Director. "But I understand. Exaggeration due to enthusiasm is certainly excusable. Anyway, I have no idea how many bird species there are in the United States and Canada."

"Well," admitted Frank Lutz, "neither do I. But I assure you that more than five hundred different kinds of insects live in or come to our seventy-five by two-hundred-foot lot."

"Now," said Dr. Lucas, "I know that you are exaggerating. That is a lot of insects."

"I agree," replied the curator, "whether you mean 'many' or are making a pun. Listen. If the museum will agree to raise my salary by ten dollars a year for every species above five hundred that I honestly find on our lot, I shall agree to have my salary reduced by ten dollars a year for every species short of five hundred."

The bargain was not made, although the curator's earnestness eventually produced a small increase in the entomology department staff. But Lutz became curious about the validity of his wager, and started wondering how many insects he really might find in his garden.

There was nothing extra special about his own backyard in New Jersey. It was an average size. It was in a typical suburban community. It was, in short, like countless other suburban yards all over the United States.

That evening when he got home, Lutz went out into the yard with his net. Within a few brief minutes he had over 20 different insects—including a butterfly, a moth, three bees, a yellow jacket, and several ants. Carefully he went through all the procedures of preparation, drying his insects, laying out the winged ones on the spreading board, writing a label for each, and finally pinning them all neatly into a cork-lined box. The backyard collection had begun.

This small-game hunting around the lot was to be continued—off and on—for the next three years. It was a very leisurely kind of hunt, one of many sparetime projects he had going. But from the start, he did keep to certain strict rules.

No special tricks were to be used to attract more insects—not even that old standby of "sugaring for moths," that is, spreading a sugary mixture or syrup onto a tree to attract moths. Nor would he make a special pond in the garden. This meant losing out on some aquatic bugs and beetles, even though these can fly. He never did come across, for instance, any water-striders, those fascinating creatures that skate so expertly on water, or water boatmen, or comical back-swimmers. But the yard was visited by other aquatic species—among them whirling beetles, large diving beetles, and even one or two giant waterbugs.

In fact, an aquatic insect was among the first to come to a trap he had attached to the porch light to catch moths and other light-loving insects that flew to it (the trap he'd allowed because it wasn't luring new insects, simply catching those that were there). It turned out to be a caddis fly, one of his favorite insects.

A few years before he had spent some enjoyable weeks at the Mount Desert Island Biological Laboratory in Maine doing work with caddis fly larvae. These are funny little caterpillar-like creatures that live in water. They have a most unusual trait: they build cases around their bodies in which they live. Each species, moreover, makes a different kind of case. One species uses grains of sand, another works with tiny pebbles and a third with little twigs cemented together with a kind of silk. Lutz had decided to see what would happen if the larvae couldn't get their normal material

—if, for instance, a twig user was taken out of its "log cabin" case and given only sea sand to work with. A whole series of different tests were tried with different species. The little creatures, he found, were amazingly adaptable. Confronted with building material they had never seen before they would nevertheless go right ahead and make do with whatever was at hand. Usually they were surprisingly successful.

The adult caddis fly, a moth-like creature, is air-borne. But like many other aquatic species (those that are aquatic as larvae, that is) the adult caddis fly tends to remain fairly close to water. Even so, as many as 32 different species visited the Lutz yard. There were many other aquatic insects, too, among them: stone flies, mayflies, dragonflies, dobson flies, and no less than nine different species of mosquito.

By the end of the first year alone, over 800 different insects had been recorded. Without even looking hard he would have won the bet. Not one of his specimens, moreover, was in the least bit out of the way. All were common, familiar natives, typical of that region of the United States. Most common of all were the moths, which far outnumbered other visitors. And of the moths most numerous of all were the very familiar brownish specimens belonging to the *Noctuid* family.

Other old friends, too, came to call. He counted at least six species of *Drosophila*, still a favorite laboratory companion of his. He was working on some endurance tests involving *Drosophila melanogaster* even then, and the creatures proved amazingly hardy. It was part of a series of experiments that he had started on a few months before. Another entomologist, E. P. Felt, had visited him, and told him of some tests he had been making on insects and altitude. Felt had attached insect traps to kites and then sent them up as far as they could go. The traps had caught an astonishing number and variety of insects—even some wingless ones! None of them, moreover, had been any the worse for their flight.

This was just the kind of tidbit to whet Lutz's curiosity. Everybody knew winds could carry insects great distances and air currents lift them up to great heights. But how high could they be carried—and still survive? Nobody had the slightest idea.

It would, Lutz now decided, be very interesting to try to find out. He had just been doing some experiments with a *Spirobolus,* a kind of millipede (not, strictly speaking, an insect, although a near relative), on the relation between temperature and walking speed. For that test he had invented a remarkably ingenious and delicately balanced "walking wheel." He had found that the warmer the temperature became, the faster the creature walked. Now, after what Felt had told him, he knew exactly what his next test would be—he would try to find out what effect altitude might have on walking speed.

He took a *Spirobolus* and the "walking wheel" to the laboratory of a physicist friend, where he put them into a large bell jar to which a vacuum pump was attached. He could now decrease or increase the air pressure in the jar by pumping air out of it or into it. Thus he could simulate the air pressure at different levels above and below sea level. Both temperature and humitidy, however, would be kept constant.

The *Spirobolus* was now all set for its "flight." He checked the barometric gauge in the bell jar. It read 740 millimeters, the normal air pressure for this particular location since the laboratory was in a mountain region a few hundred feet above sea level. He started pumping, taking air out of the jar.

Quickly the air pressure level dropped to 500 mm. — the equivalent of about two miles above sea level. Lutz stopped the pump now and checked the *Spirobolus*. All thousand legs were treading the walking wheel in perfect, regular rhythm, obviously completely undisturbed by what had just happened.

Now he pumped the pressure down to 400 mm. The legs moved just a tiny fraction faster, but that was all. Yet man at this level—even if the change had been made more gradually—would already be suffering the effects of thin air and lack of oxygen. His breathing would be labored, his walk a little wobbly.

Another interval of three or four minutes and down again the air pressure went: first to 300 mm., then a pause, next to 250 mm., another pause, and then down to 200 mm. The *Spirobolus* was higher now than Mount Everest. Yet, amazing creature, it was now actually walking faster than when it started. Man by now would be dead—unable to survive any length of time at such altitudes without the aid of oxygen or other special apparatus.

Astonished by the creature's toughness, Lutz started the pump again. Down the air pressure level dropped, lower and lower and lower until it was all the way down to 22mm.

"That was as far as we went," Lutz noted. The

water in the jar had just about reached its vapor pressure level. "It seemed far enough for the present," he added.

It certainly was. Within less than one hour the *Spirobolus* had been shot from the equivalent of sea level to a height of 17 miles above the earth. No man had —then—ever been up so high. Man—without some artificial aid—wouldn't have stood a chance, even five minutes after the start of the test. But this remarkable creature had survived it all. True, after the seven-mile level it had slowed down. Now at the 17-mile level (there was practically no air left) it had stopped moving. Yet when Lutz started pumping air back into the jar, the tiny legs started moving again almost immediately. He pumped in more air until the pressure returned to normal. By this time, the *Spirobolus* was walking away as busily as ever. It looked, Lutz though, well enough to stand a second "flight."

"Now we went to 100 mm. and back to normal," Lutz noted. "We repeated this round trip three more times—all in two hours and a half."

Wonder of wonders, the *Spirobolus* was still alive and walking. Even Lutz was so impressed he was moved to comment: "Of what stuff are these creatures made?"

Then he decided to try the test on *Drosophila*. Ten of them went into a bell jar together with a small container of water. Lutz pumped quickly and in 90 seconds the air was practically all gone.

Had it been too much? There was not one sign of life. But then, as he watched, one twitched slightly. Four minutes later, he noted with relief, "all ten were walking about as though nothing had happened."

Again and again he put them through the same ordeal: from normal air pressure to practically none in a minute and a half. After the twentieth time, only six out of the ten flies were still alive. After the twenty-fourth, only one male and one female survived. It was enough.

"There seemed no point in pushing the experiment to their death," he reported later. "Besides I wanted to see if they were really as well and hearty as they seemed to be. So, I put them in a cage with a nice ripe banana, where they started breeding the next day. Careful microscopic examination of their children, grandchildren and great-grandchildren failed to reveal indications that anything unusual in fruit-fly affairs had happened."

It was astounding. Yet even their endurance must have a limit. What was it, Lutz wondered. They had survived easily in fantastically thin air. Could they survive in no air at all? In a vacuum?

Impossible, one of the physicists at the laboratory insisted. As he watched Lutz go ahead with the preparations (two solitary bees, two ants, one young grasshopper, and a beetle would make the "trip"), he jokingly suggested a lot of time and trouble would be saved by simply stepping on the insects. It would be a much easier, quicker way of killing them than Lutz's bizarre scheme.

But Lutz went right on with his arrangements. Finally, his six "passengers" safely inside a special tube he had set up, he was ready to start pumping. Within two minutes a complete vacuum had been reached. He checked his watch—he would wait for 60 seconds.

Then he broke the tube. Thus within one instant, the insects went from a complete vacuum to normal air—the first insects in history to make that most unusual trip.

Of the six passengers, one—an ant—died the following day. The other five survivors flourished, not a bit the worse for their ordeal.

Other endurance tests followed. A cricket was subjected to air pressure at the 2,300-mm. mark—three times that of normal—and survived, without any of the lengthy decompression procedures man must have. It was plunged into a centrifuge and whirled around for 10 minutes at the tremendous rate of 1,200 revolutions per minute. It survived that, too.

"All I can say," wrote Lutz when he completed the series of tests, "is that insects seem to be better made than we are. They have invaded almost every bit of the livable world, including hot springs, and the highest mountains, the Arctic and the tropics, in water and on water, underground and above ground, in plants and animals and on them."

And some unexpected ones had invaded his backyard, too. One day during the second summer of his survey, Lutz could hardly believe his eyes when he saw a certain insect dipping unconcernedly into his petunias, looking completely at home. But it was indeed a *Euglossid,* a curious-looking tropical bee with a tongue so long it trails along under the entire length of the body and sticks out behind like a tail! Never had a *Euglossid* been seen any further north than Mexico. How this one found its way to New Jersey, Lutz would never know for certain, although

he suspected that it may have been hidden in a tropical plant imported here from South America. In any case it went in together with the other bees found in the yard (the total reached 73 different species) where it lent an exotic, tropical touch to the collection.

By the end of the third summer, Lutz decided to bring his backyard safari to a close. He knew the census was still far from complete. Many species, he knew, must have escaped his attention—it had been a very casual safari. Still others, though perfectly common to the region, had simply never visited his particular yard. To his sorrow the collection lacked, for instance, that green-tailed beauty of the night, the luna moth. He had seen these splendid creatures on occasion in neighbors' yards. But not one, as far as he knew, had visited his.

If he continued the hunt, and worked harder at it, he knew his collection would grow bigger. But he felt that he had already more than justified the seemingly bold claim he'd made to Dr. Lucas.

By December 1938, the grand total stood at 1,402 different insect species. Of that total, there were 432 species of moths, 35 varieties of butterflies, 259 kinds of beetles, 258 *Diptera* (flies, mosquitoes, and their relatives), 167 species of *Hymenoptera* (bees, wasps, and ants), 75 different homopterous insects (that is, the leafhoppers, aphids, and scale insects), and 62 different true bugs.

Even though he never got the salary increase he'd proposed to Dr. Lucas, he had gotten a lot of fun out of his backyard safari. His collection became the focus of an attractive new exhibit at the Museum, called "Insects of a Suburban Yard."

He got something else out of that conversation with Dr. Lucas which had started the whole thing. He got the title for a book that he wrote about his insect visitors. *A Lot of Insects* (pun intended) would show readers how exciting it can be to study their own backyards. It would also carry on his crusade for more human tolerance of the insect world.

When the suburban yard exhibit was put on view at the Museum, people kept asking him, "But what does your yard look like with all those insects in it? It must be an awful place!"

In his book he answered them, explaining that his yard was not being depleted of plants or full of weeds and insect pests as he knew they suspected. In fact, his yard had actually won several prizes in garden contests, during the very years in which he was making his insect survey.

Then he reminded his readers that he had preserved only one sample of each type of insect visitor, and let the rest go on about their business as always.

"Now I will ask a question," he wrote in the last paragraph of his book. "Do you still think, if you ever did, that insects as a whole are bad? I sometimes wonder if the percentage of 'good neighbors' among humans is as large."

There would never be a time when Frank Lutz would feel differently about his backyard creatures. His "lot of insects" would remain his "good neighbors" forever.

Nature Projects You Can Do

The student of insect life enjoys a great advantage: insects are all around us. They may be found, as Dr. Lutz often said, "everywhere and at all times." In the city or the country, in an apartment or a one-family house, in a suburban backyard, a town dump, or a city park, there is always an abundant supply of insect life.

There is never-ending fascination in the study of the strange and wondrous ways of insects: their food habits, life cycles, social relationships, home-building skills, and other interesting traits. Moreover, while we already know much about insect life, much, much more remains to be learned. Even the amateur entomologist can make a contribution to science through his own research results in a particular field.

1. Your Basic Equipment

According to Dr. Lutz, the most essential items for insect students are "an inquiring mind, eyes and fingers." In addition to these, certain material items will be necessary. But the beginning entomologist is doubly fortunate. Not only is his subject matter handy wherever he may be, but the equipment he needs is inexpensive and, in many cases, easily made. Most of the things you will need will be described as they are called for in the projects below. But before going very far with any of these projects, there are three things you should have first.

Your nature notebook will be indispensable. In it you will record your observations of insect activity. If you see an ant colony battling, a butterfly emerging from a chrysalis, ladybug beetles devouring plant lice—write it down in your nature notebook. Perhaps you will make a Backyard Survey (project 7) as did Dr. Lutz; your notebook will be a constant companion.

Perhaps you will keep an Insect Zoo (project 8), or just a single variety for observation; in your notebook you will be able to keep track of such details as feeding times and events in the life cycles of your pets. A small spiral pad, or perhaps a pocket-size looseleaf notebook, will be a good choice.

A field guide will aid you in identifying the insects you encounter. It will also tell you such things as their preferred nesting places and food plants, so that you will know where to search for a specific variety, and what to feed it when you have caught it. Dr. Lutz's *Field Book of Insects* is one of several such guides that may be bought at your bookstore or borrowed from the library.

A magnifying glass will enable you to get a close look at an insect's structure, and will help you to locate identifying features that may be hard to see with the naked eye. A folding pocket magnifier, perhaps one that has two lenses of different magnification, is a good choice, but a more simple glass will also do.

2. Looking for Insects

Why look? Perhaps you are planning to start an ant colony for your Insect Zoo; or perhaps you wish to photograph as many kinds of insect "homes" as possible. Perhaps you have heard of the presence of an unusual variety in your neighborhood, as did the young Frank Lutz when his father came upon a hill full of walking sticks. Perhaps you are making an insect survey of your own backyard, or the playground or parking lot near your school. And you might even discover something that will make the world of science sit up and take notice of you: possibly a new species, but more likely a known variety in a place where it has never been observed before, or doing something nobody ever knew it did.

Where to look. Insects are literally everywhere: on sand, under rocks, at or below the surface of ponds or rivers, in the cold Arctic or the dry desert, in logs, under moss, on leaves and tree trunks, in garden and farm soil, on city streets, in the mud of riverbanks, in barnyards and haystacks, at the seashore, in and about every type of plant from trees to algae and from rose bushes to sagebrush, near stagnant water and old animal bones, and even in our very homes.

When to look. Insects are present at every season, but in different forms. Study your field guide to know what stage of development you may expect to find at a given time of year. For most species, fall, winter, and early spring are the times you can find eggs and pupae; from spring through the end of summer both larvae and adults will be about. Insects may be found in the daytime or at night; some species are more active at night, while others prefer the sun, and still others seek out dark places for their daytime spurt of activity. Warm bright days and hot, humid, cloudy or moonless nights are good times for spotting activity of diurnal and nocturnal varieties.

3. Bringing Insects to You

You can make use of the fact that certain insects are attracted to certain plants or to light. Keep a record of your baiting activities, and their results, in your notebook.

By *planting* flowers, tree, vegetables, and shrubs that are liked by insects, you can increase the insect population of your garden. Apple, elm, maple, willow trees; honeysuckle, lilac, marigolds, verbena, zinnias; carrots, cucumbers, squash, tomatoes—these and many others are possibilities. Remember, without insecticides, and with over 1400 species of insects, Lutz's garden still took prizes in a garden contest.

Sugaring is particularly useful in attracting nocturnal varieties. You will need *a*) a pint of molasses, some brown sugar, and some stale fruit juice, mixed together and allowed to stand in a warm place for several hours, or *b*) over-ripe fruit, such as bananas, peaches, or plums, rubbed through a sieve, mashed, or pureed in an electric blender, mixed with brown sugar, and allowed to stand in a warm place for a day or two until fermented. A paint brush and pail, and some white or luminous adhesive tape complete your equipment. The time to sugar is just at twilight on a warm, humid, cloudy night.

109

The ideal place would be a thicket of trees, a forest path, the outskirts of a woods—an area small enough so that you can walk over it in about 20 minutes. Paint a dab of your sugaring mixture on tree trunks at a convenient height, at intervals of 20 or 30 feet. Mark the trees with adhesive tape so you will be able to find them easily later. After you have completed painting the area you have selected, return to the beginning and get your flashlight, net and collecting jars (see project 5). Just after dusk, retrace your steps over the sugared trail, stopping at each tree and picking or tapping the insects off the baited bark and into your jars. Repeat the tour several times more, and you will surely have a good supply of specimens to sort and mount in the days ahead.

Light is attractive to moths in particular and many other nocturnal creatures as well. Even a porch light, a lamp in an apartment window, or the headlight of a car can be the beginning of an effective light trap. Armed with a net, you can capture many of the creatures it attracts. But an old white bedsheet suspended near or behind the source of light will really help. It intensifies the effect of the light by reflecting it, and the insects will fly into the sheet, where you can easily see them. Turn up the bottom of the sheet for a foot or so and pin it at the sides to make a loose pocket that rests on the ground. Many crawling species will be trapped in this pocket. Or you can set the sheet directly on the ground, and place a lantern in the middle of it.

Many simple *traps* will help you in your search. Put some of the sugaring mixture or a piece of spoiled meat into a clean glass jar and sink it into the ground, its top level with the surface of the ground. By tilting a slab of wood or stone across the mouth of the jar you can keep out rain and delude the ground-crawling insects into thinking they have found a safe place to hide. Make sure there is a way for the insects to get in, and check your traps every other day. Or you can wrap a strip of an old bedsheet or cheesecloth around the trunk of a tree in the autumn, when cooler weather sends insects looking for a warm corner in which to hibernate. Or you can place

110

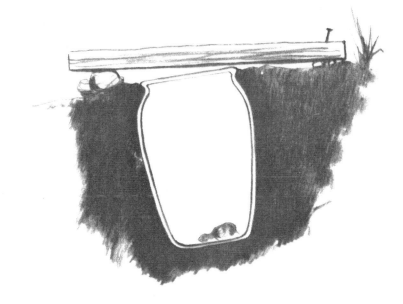

a dead mouse, a raw hamburger patty, or a bone with some meat still on it on the ground. Cover this bait with a slab of stone or wood, and check in a day or so to see what you have attracted.

4. Catching the Insects

Probably the most familiar piece of insect-catching equipment is the butterfly net or *aerial net*, used not only for capturing butterflies but for every type of flying creature: moths, true flies, dragonflies, wasps, and bees, among others. Use an aerial net in open country, along the roadside, at a beach, or in a field or garden.

It is easy to make. You will need: a strong piece of $^3/_{16}$ or $^1/_4$-inch wire, about $3^1/_2$ feet long; a stick or handle about 3 feet long; adhesive tape; a piece of open mesh nylon, cheesecloth or mosquito netting (even a gauzy type of window curtain might be used—the color doesn't matter) about $1^1/_4$ yards long and 1 yard wide; a strip of stronger fabric, such as unbleached muslin, 1 yard long and 4 inches wide, and a needle and thread.

Bend the wire to form a hoop about 12 inches in diameter, twist the ends together where they meet, and bend them at right angles to the hoop. Smooth the stick or handle with sandpaper. Tape the wire ends firmly to one end of the handle (or fasten them more firmly by drilling two holes near the end of the handle and passing the wires through in opposite directions; then bind with tape or strong twine). To cut the fabric for the bag, first make a paper pattern following the sketch, opposite. Then fold the fabric in half, pin the pattern on it, and cut. Pin and sew the two pieces together about $1/2$ inch from the edge, leaving the top open, to form a bag about $1\frac{1}{2}$ times as long as it is wide. A back stitch or a combination running-back stitch will hold the seam securely. Then sew the seam edges down into the body of the net, using an overcasting stitch. Next, pin the long strip of strong fabric to the top of your net bag, and join one edge of this band to the top edge of the net in a half-inch seam. Place the bag inside the hoop. Fold the band down over the hoop, turn the edge under and use an overcasting stitch to sew it to the seam joining the band and the net bag.

Practice in using your net will teach you the most effective way. Once you have netted a specimen, a quick flip of the net bag over the rim will keep it locked in until you can transfer it to your collecting jar. It will take practice to get the insect out of the net and into the jar. After it is trapped, tuck the handle under your arm. That frees both hands to get the collecting jar, open it, and place it in the net, as close to the trapped insect as possible. Then tap or drop the specimen into the jar. Larger butterflies may be quieted by giving them a quick pinch with the thumb and forefinger on the sides of the thorax (behind the head, under the winds) with the wings up over the back.

A *sweeping net* is used in overgrown, grassy areas, or through brush or dense foliage. It is made the same way, only of stronger fabric, such as lightweight unbleached muslin. It is not necessary to add the top band. The handle can be shorter and stouter. If, like many good entomologists, you do not

112

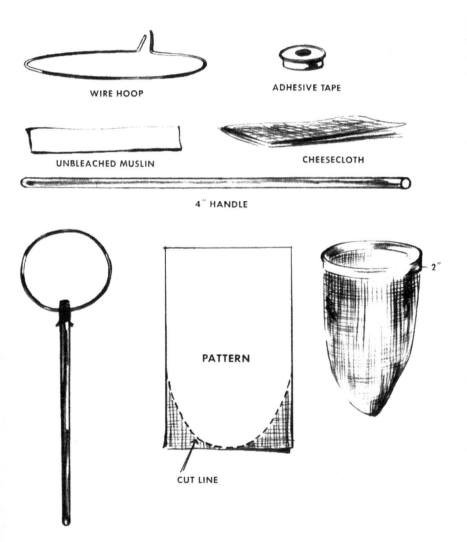

WIRE HOOP

ADHESIVE TAPE

UNBLEACHED MUSLIN

CHEESECLOTH

4″ HANDLE

PATTERN

CUT LINE

2″

want to be bothered with extra equipment, one sturdy net will do for aerial netting as well as sweeping. Use the net by literally sweeping it through the grass or foliage from left to right and then from right to left in a zigzag pattern, keeping the open side of the net forward with a twist of your wrist. Spiders, beetles, leafhoppers, and grasshoppers are among the rich harvest you will get with a sweeping net. You will also get plenty of leaves, twigs, dirt, and other debris; but your insects will crawl up to the top of the net where they can be picked off and placed in your collecting jars.

Beating is the method used to get insects out of trees and bushes. You will need only a large stick and your net. Hold the net open under the branch of a likely-looking tree. Whack the branch firmly with the stick, and collect the insects that drop into the net. Any piece of cloth spread on the ground under the tree can be used to collect the insects as they fall. Almost any trees—even dead ones, but especially those in full bloom—will prove rewarding.

5. *The Hows of Collecting*

Dry killing is used for most of the creatures you will collect: hard-bodied insects, caterpillars, and such scaly or hairy ones as butterflies, moths, and true flies. A safe killing jar for such creatures may be easily prepared. Several 4-ounce or smaller wide-mouthed jars with tight-fitting covers (small baby-food or peanut-butter jars would be good), water, a pound of plaster of paris, masking tape, and 8 ounces of carbon tetrachloride (common cleaning fluid sold under various trade names) are the items you will need.
tetrachloride (common cleaning fluid sold under various trade names) are the items you will need.

Clean the jars thoroughly, and let dry. Pour about 1/3 cup of water into bowl. Spoon dry plaster of paris on top of the water until all the plaster is wet and almost all of the water is absorbed. Then stir slowly so that no lumps remain and no air bubbles are formed. Pour the wet plaster mixture into the glass jars to make a layer of about 3/4 inch at the

114

bottom, and let stand until set. (Clean mixing bowl and spoon while plaster is still wet, and discard scraps of plaster in an old newspaper.) When the plaster in the jars is almost dry, wipe splashes off the sides of the jars; if necessary, scrape gently with a dull knife and wipe clean with a dry cloth. Write "insect killing jar" on strips of masking tape and attach one to each jar. Leave the jars about 24 hours or until the plaster is completely dry. Just before you set out on your collecting trip, pour just enough carbon tetrachloride into the jars to saturate the plaster. Cover tightly so that the fluid does not evaporate. Tear up some strips of soft paper to line the jars with, so that the specimens will not be injured as you walk around. Now the jars are ready to use.

You will need a *storage box* if you are on a field trip of even several hours' duration, or if you will not be able to mount your specimens the same day. Insects should not be left in the dry-killing jar for too long, or the fumes may cause discoloration and the creatures may become bruised. After a half hour they will surely be dead. A strong metal or plastic pocket-size box is good for field storage of specimens. It should be fitted with layers of tissue or glazed cotton such as jewelry is packed in (never use ordinary cotton, as the fibers will cling to the insects), and some paradichlorobenzene crystals (moth flakes) should be placed under the bottom layer just in case a specimen starts coming to life. Pack the storage box from the bottom up, placing each specimen on its own bed of cotton. Always keep all the cotton in the box when it is closed, to prevent the insects from sliding around. When your field trip is over, open the storage boxes and leave in a warm place for several days to make sure your specimens have dried out. After they are dry, some more paradichlorobenzene sprinkled on top will protect them from insect-eating pests until you are ready to sort and mount them. Close the boxes and store in a larger, tightly covered metal container until you are ready.

To "bring 'em back alive," some small metal or plastic containers will do. Put a few leaves, a twig, or even a slightly damp piece of paper toweling into the box—use enough leaves or paper to fill the box so that the insect has something to cling to and will not be bounced around. Some earth-dwelling creatures will be happy with a mound of earth; take ants with the earth in which you find them.

Triangular envelopes are used for storing moths and butterflies, whose delicate colored scales will be damaged if they are even touched with a greasy finger or placed in a killing jar with other types of insects. For this reason you should keep one killing jar for *Lepidoptera* alone. These insects should be handled with forceps only, preferably a smooth, broad type. Triangular envelopes can be made easily by folding a rectangular piece of paper as shown in the diagram. Be sure to write the date and place you have collected your butterfly on the outside of the envelope before you put the insect inside. When you put it inside, fold the wings back carefully over its back.

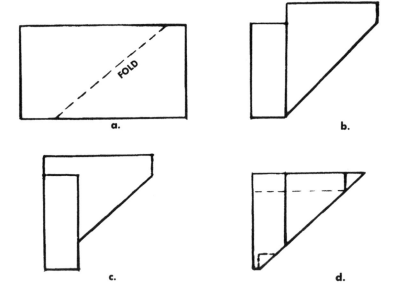

a. b.

c. d.

Wet killing is used for soft-bodied creatures, including spiders, most eggs, larvae, and pupae, a few beetles, and anything microscopically tiny. Small jars or vials, such as test tubes, are filled 2/3 full with 70% ethyl rubbing alcohol, and closed tightly with cork plugs. When collecting insects for wet killing, use a camel's-hair paint brush dipped into the alcohol to dislodge the desired insect from the leaf on which it is perched; then "wash" the brush off in the collecting vial and the insect will remain. Do not crowd too many specimens or groups in one jar. If you cannot get small vials and are using larger jars, tie each group of specimens in a little bag of cheesecloth to keep them separate; or use wads of paper to separate one group from another as you collect them.

Labels should be placed with everything you collect, as soon as you collect. Place, date, and variety, if known, should be noted on a small piece of paper and placed in the killing jars and storage boxes with each insect.

Dr. Lutz's *Field Book of Insects* describes additional collecting techniques.

6. *Preserving and Mounting*

Most of the insects you will collect have been dry-killed, and should now be *pinned and mounted*. You will need: insect pins (not the regular sewing kind; these are longer, more slender, and stronger, and must be obtained from a biological supply house); forceps for handling small or fragile forms; some stiff white paper (index cards will do); scissors; ballpoint pen; white shellac.

Perhaps your specimens have gotten quite hard in their storage box; you will need a relaxing box before you can mount them. This is a sort of humidifier, made out of a tobacco tin, cookie tin, plastic refrigerator box, aquarium, or similar container. It must be water-tight and able to be covered. Put a 1½-inch layer of some porous material on the bottom—sand, balsa wood, synthetic sponge would do—and saturate with water. Sprinkle with paradichlorobenzene, and cover with a layer of paper toweling. Put your specimens into the relaxing box on the paper in their storage wrappings or envelopes. Do not fill the box to the top. Place some soft cloth or paper toweling across the opening of the box to absorb excess moisture, and cover. Most insects will relax in 24 hours, although some very large ones may take longer. Relax only those specimens you will be able to work on in a day. It is not a good idea to leave insects in the relaxing box for more than three days, as they may disintegrate or get discolored.

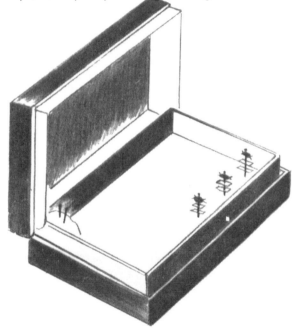

Mounting boxes are used for storing and displaying your collection. Make your own out of a deep cigar box, preferably a wooden one. Line with sheet cork, balsa wood, or two layers of corrugated cardboard placed so that the corrugations are at right angles. Glue the lining material firmly in place. If you paint the box white, inside and out, your specimens will show up nicely; be sure the paint is completely dry before you use the box, or else you will spoil your collection.

BUMBLEBEE

SIX-SPOTTED TIGER BEETLE

**COMMON SULPHUR
BUTTERFLY**

SMALL INSECTS

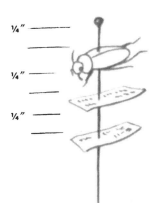

¼" ——

¼" ——

¼" ——

**METHODS OF
MOUNTING DIFFERENT
INSECTS**

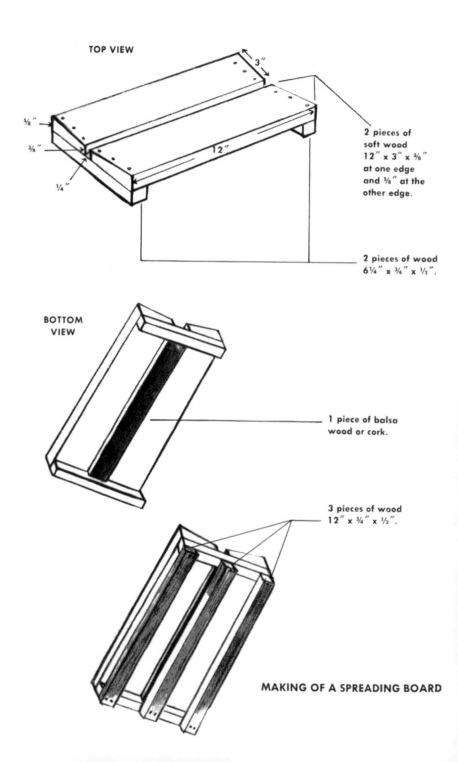

TOP VIEW

3″

⅝″

¾″

¼″

12″

2 pieces of
soft wood
12″ x 3″ x ⅜″
at one edge
and ⅝″ at the
other edge.

2 pieces of wood
6¼″ x ¾″ x ½″.

BOTTOM
VIEW

1 piece of balsa
wood or cork.

3 pieces of wood
12″ x ¾″ x ½″.

MAKING OF A SPREADING BOARD

Guide strips of
strong letter paper
7″ long and 3⁄16″ wide.

Glass headed furriers'
pins. (Each specimen
needs about 10 for
mounting.)

Steel insect pins.
(Number 3 is the
most generally used.)

Spreading needles.
Use Number 11 or 12
sewing needle with
wooden match sticks
for handles.

**MATERIALS FOR USING
SPREADING BOARD**

Now you are ready to pin your specimens. Remove one at a time from the relaxing box. Using forceps, magnifying glass, and field guide, identify your specimens as closely as possible. Insert the pin straight through the body of the insect, from top to underside, slightly to the right of the insect's center and slightly forward, as shown in the illustrations. The exact spot for pinning varies with the different orders. Beetles, for instance, are pinned through the right-wing cover; bees and flies through the thorax, slightly to the right of center; butterflies, moths, and dragonflies are pinned through the center of the thorax. These last three groups should be mounted with their wings spread out flat. (A *spreading board* is used to set the wings of these creatures in the proper position. See the illustration for details of how to construct and use one.) Leave 1/3 inch of pin length above the insect. Below the insect you will pin two labels; a locality label, telling where you found the specimen, the date, and your name; and the name label, giving the specimen's genus, species, and, if possible, the name of the authority who first identified it (try to find this information in your field guide). Write the labels neatly, in letters as small as possible, on small pieces of stiff white paper, about 1/2-by-1 inch in size, and place on the pin so that about 1/4 inch of space is between insect, locality label, and name label, with somewhat more than 1/4 inch of pin left over at the bottom. Now push the pinned insect neatly into place in the mounting box.

To mount very small insects, cut paper "points" from an index card. These are isosceles triangles with a base of 1/8 inch and a length of 3/8 inch. Push an insect pin through the point near the base and bend the point slightly near the apex. Put a drop of white shellac on this tip, and touch the underneath right side of the insect with it. Let dry, and label and mount as above.

Do not crowd your specimens, or they will not look good. If you have a large collection, keep each group in a separate box. Or a box can tell a story, such as "One day of Insect Hunting in the Park" with a representative selection of what you found;

122

"From an Aerial (or Sweeping) Net"; "Insects from our Maple Trees"; or "Life Cycle of the---," which might contain eggs, larvae, pupae, and male and female adults of a species, as well as dried samples of the insect's preferred food plant, possibly its home, and, of course, appropriate labels.

When your mounting box is arranged to your satisfaction, it should be left open in a warm dry place for several days to dry out the specimens thoroughly. A teaspoonful of para-dichlorobenzene, sprinkled in the box, or tied in a small cheesecloth bag and placed in the box, will provide protection. The cover of the box should fit snugly. If desired, get a pane of window glass cut to the top dimensions of your box and tape it neatly into place along the edges, so that your specimens can be seen while the box is sealed.

Soft-bodied creatures that have been wet-killed should be *preserved in liquid*. The same 70% ethyl alcohol as was used for killing them is also used as the preserving fluid. It should be changed once at first, and afterwards only if it becomes discolored. Each insect should have its own small vial, labeled.

7. Backyard Survey

After you have tried a few brief collecting trips, and had the experience of drying and mounting specimens, you will be ready for a more extensive project. How about an insect survey of your backyard, such as Dr. Lutz made? He never resorted to sugaring or any other kind of baiting, but just collecting representatives of the species that he noticed, casually, over three years. One day he might be waiting for lunch when an unusual bee, buzzing around the petunias near the door, caught his eye, and wound up in his net. Another time he heard a chirping coming from the fireplace: an English cricket had come to visit. Nocturnal species were attracted by the regular porch light.

Your survey may be made over a summer season, or at intervals during the year, or even over several years. Keep a record of your finds by date; mount them by species. Kill

123

only what you need—one adult male and one female of each species should do in most cases—or else your collection will be more redundant than informative.

If you do not have a backyard, a nearby vacant lot or a city park are good substitutes. Perhaps you can "borrow" the yard of a friend or relative whom you visit regularly. And a portion of your school grounds or summer camp can provide a hunting territory for a group of interested junior entomologists.

8. An Insect Zoo

A few specimens of even one variety of insect can be the beginning of a fascinating zoo. The entomologist is lucky among zoologists in that, for the most part, his charges require little space, little food, and little attention. Once a species has been set up properly in a cage with food and whatever else it may require, the insect-keeper can just sit back and enjoy watching the activity that takes place. Several suggestions for species that are easy to acquire and keep are given here:

Fruit flies will come readily to a jar baited with a few slices of ripe, even overripe, banana. Choose a 1/2-pint jar such as mayonnaise or preserves come in, or a large peanut-butter jar, and clean it thoroughly. Drop in the banana, and leave the open jar out of doors, preferably during the summer or early autumn, until a few flies have congregated. Since they breed rapidly, quite a large colony will result. Place a piece of dry paper toweling in the jar to give the flies and their maggots a "foothold," plug the jar with a large wad of cotton, and your colony has begun. A new generation will appear every two weeks or so, and the flies will continue to breed until their food supply is all gone or until mold finally attacks them. Fruit flies will go to light, and you can transfer them to a new container of the same size by covering the old one with dark cloth, putting the two container openings together, and holding near a strong light.

Crickets can be kept in a large aquarium covered with a

124

pane of glass. Be sure to leave a small opening for air—but not large enough to allow the crickets to escape. Give them a bottom layer of about 2 inches of soft soil or sand, and keep it slightly moist but never too wet. Add a few stones, and perhaps a clump of earth with wild plants and decaying leaves. A small vial filled with water and tightly plugged with a wad of cotton will provide drinking water for your cricket pets. Or a wet piece of crumpled newspaper will provide shelter as well as drink. Feed them bread crumbs, lettuce shreds, pieces of hard-boiled egg or apple or even dog biscuit. Remove uneaten food at least every other day; do not feed too much at a time. Keep only one species in a cage; if mixed, they will fight bitterly. Large cricket colonies need cages of wire mesh with a wooden frame to provide enough space. Males, not females, "sing" by rubbing their wings together. Eggs are laid in the earth, and the baby crickets hatch looking like adults without wings. Watch your cricket pets develop.

Ants are also easy to keep, and a variety of containers may be used. One of the simplest consists of two big, wide-mouthed glass jars of different sizes, so that one nests inside the other, leaving about a half-inch of space between them. Fill this space with earth, pushing a piece of tubing to the bottom of the jar. You can add water through this tube so that the earth near the bottom will be damp, while the top part is dry. If your inner jar is shorter than the outer one, it will serve as a feeding chamber. Anchor one end of a piece of ribbon or string in the earth and let the other end hang down to the bottom of the food chamber. This will serve as a "ladder" to let the ants get to their food. Feed them small quantities of cheese, apple, bread, gum drops, and anything else you want to try. Keep a record of what they like. Fit some fine mesh or netting—even an old nylon stocking—over the top of the jar and secure it with two or three rubber bands. You will be able to watch the ants tunneling through the earth be-tween the jars. They prefer to do their work in the dark, so keep this nest in a dark room, or cover it with a piece of dark cloth.

Caterpillars are easy to care for, and with luck and patience you can watch them grow into adult butterflies or moths. The caterpillars, or larvae, can be kept in any dry clean box or jar, covered with cloth or wire mesh or netting. Observe what the caterpillar is feeding on, so that you can provide the proper food. The leaves of the food plant should be fresh. You can either pot an entire plant or place its stems in a small bottle of water. Make sure that the bottle opening around the stems is packed tightly with cotton, so that the insect does not fall into the water and drown. You can now place the bottle on its side in your cage without danger of spilling. Wrap a strip of cloth or paper toweling around the bottle, so that the caterpillar can climb easily: glass surfaces are sometimes too slippery. Replace the plant as the leaves are eaten; if it appears wilted, add new stems and fresh water.

126

A simple cage for rearing caterpillars can be made with wire mesh or screening, rolled into a cylinder and fastened with cord or wire. Close it at both ends with the lids of tin cans, ice cream containers, or plastic jar tops (the plastic lids of coffee tins would be good). Put in your potted food plant or bottle of foliage, and the caterpillar, and watch what happens as the days pass.

Once the caterpillar has reached its full growth, it will lose interest in its food. This means it is ready to pupate. Some species spin their cocoons or form their chrysalids above ground; these will attach themselves to a twig if you provide one. Other species go underground to pupate; provide an inch or two of soft damp earth at the bottom of the cage for these, and make sure to keep it damp. The duration of the pupal stage varies greatly, depending on species and temperature. But try, particularly if you have an above-ground pupa, to be there for the "coming-out party." It is a splendid sight to behold.

You will probably not be able to keep an adult butterfly or moth confined for very long, unless you can provide a very large airy cage. Some diluted honey or sugar syrup can be given them. poured on a small sponge in a shallow dish. The large silk-spinning moths do not eat durig the adult stage.

If you are successful at keeping these insect pets, you may be able to add other varieties as well. Spiders, mantids, meal worms (the larvae of a beetle), and aquatic insects seen near the surface of a pond are some other possibilities for your insect zoo.